Eat Spendidly Anytime Without Losing Your Mind

by Cheryl Merser

A Fireside Book Published by Simon & Schuster
New York   London   Toronto   Sydney   Tokyo   Singapore

Fireside
Rockefeller Center
1230 Avenue of the Americas
New York, NY 10020

DESIGNED BY BONNI LEON-BERMAN

Manufactured in the United States of America

10 9 8 7 6 5 4 3 2 1

Library of Congress Cataloging-in-Publication Data

Merser, Cheryl.
Relax! it's only dinner:
eat splendidly anytime without losing your mind / by Cheryl Merser.
p. cm.
Includes bibliographical references and index.
1. Dinners and dining. 2. Quick and easy cookery.
3. Entertaining. I. Title.
TX737.M47 1995
642—dc20 95-16553

ISBN 0-684-81166-9

This book is for Michael.

"A lack of knowledge about basic cookery can be somewhat inconvenient."

James Beard

C o n t e n t s

Contents

Contents

I n t r o d u c t i o n

$\mathcal{M}$y goal in the kitchen is simple: I want to cook well without having to learn very many new things and while spending as little time there as possible. My quest is always for recipes that require minimum effort and yield maximum praise and, since good cooking generally works the other way around, such recipes are not all that easy to come by. Over the years I've been zealous, however, in cadging such recipes from friends or creating them from scratch myself, and have found that I have enough to fill this book, with a few left over so that my friends won't know all my secrets.

Every year dozens of cookbooks are published and every year I buy my fair share, hope as usual getting the better of experience: "This one," I always think, "this one will be the cookbook I've *really* been waiting for." It never is.

This is rarely the fault of the cookbook, for cookbook writers on the whole seem generous, accomplished, and enthusiastic, presupposing fairly enough that their readers want to cook well and learn different techniques and flourishes—why else buy a new cookbook?—and won't mind spending a lot of time in the kitchen doing so. No doubt that's true for some of us but, for my part, I've come to realize that while I'm an ambitious cook, I'm also a lazy one. I'm not an adventuresome cook, the kind who takes on a recipe just because it's there. I "test" recipes in my head before I try them, and many recipes I come across never stand a chance: Too many ingredients—won't try that one. Too many steps to a particular recipe—out. A central ingredient I've never come across before or wouldn't know where to find—no, thanks. Anything with lots of egg whites beaten to peaks . . . probably not. A recipe on paper I can't imagine on a plate—no way.

Even so, in each new book I invariably earmark a few recipes I'm eager to play around with; some succeed brilliantly, though just as many disappoint. "Preparation Time: ten minutes," one such recipe promised not long ago. "Great," I thought, and set about making it on a weeknight at seven-thirty. Step one: "Soak the beans overnight." Ten minutes of intense hands-on preparation at the last minute, not counting all the other things you have to do, is what they meant, I guess, by preparation time.

My fault, for not reading the instructions through ahead of time, but still. You rarely see more sympathetic or honest instructions like: "Preparation Time: A day and a half, including shopping plus the time it takes to clean last week's leftovers from the pan you want to use, find the missing paring knife, empty (or load) the dishwasher, unearth your reading glasses so that you can read the small type, set the table, and make the rest of the dinner. . . ." Also, how does the recipe writer know that you can dice, chop, mince, mix, cook, and serve the dish in ten minutes just because he or she can?

Another recipe I came across recently, actually one from a renowned chef, sounded unusually easy and elegant: a kind of ground meat thing, sort of California-oriental in sensibility. It was made with some finely chopped and colorful vegetables, homemade chili oil, and some other stuff—including plum wine—and served as an appetizer scooped into delicate lettuce-leaf cups; iceberg lettuce makes excellent cups, the recipe advised. So I went to three liquor stores before finding plum wine (which keeps only as long as regular wine, the proprietor told me, and what on earth was I going to do within a week with an entire bottle of plum wine minus one quarter of a cup?), picked up the lettuce at the supermarket, and tried the dish that night for a few friends.

Leaf by leaf, to little avail, I took apart my lettuce, spreading the leaves all over the kitchen counter to see which were delicate and cuplike. The big outside leaves looked more like Frisbees, and the smaller ones inside were crinkly and flat—not one plausible lettuce cup, let alone the six I needed, to be found among them.

Meanwhile (there's always a "meanwhile" when you're cooking), the meat mixture was simmering along just fine, even though I'd decided against making homemade chili oil in favor of using chopped jalapeño pepper from a jar (easier!), plus a few dashes of (handier!) store-bought hot chili sesame oil. I added the plum wine just when I was told to. After it boiled down, I tasted the mixture and detected nothing plumlike, except for a faint sweetness, about it. It didn't taste bad; in the end, served on my lettuce-Frisbees, it actually tasted quite good. But I vowed that the next time I made it, which would be long after the plum wine had expired, I'd use regular wine, not plum, find a simpler (and cheaper!) way to infuse the faint trace of sweetness (fruit juice!), forget about lettuce cups, and serve it against a bed of shredded lettuce.

After a few more tinkering sessions, I ended up with a perfectly fine dish that meets the strict criteria for inclusion in this book: It's relatively easy, relatively foolproof, stylish, and tasty enough to suggest that you're a pretty good cook whether you are or not.

Like many of us, I grew up strong and healthy eating things like Spam, Jell-O in primary colors with bananas floating in it, tuna-noodle casserole, and (for special occasions) a memorable side dish composed of string beans doused in cream of mushroom soup with canned onion rings sprinkled lavishly on top. In its time and in its way this cuisine had a certain I'm-not-sure-what, and the memory of it remains, at least for those of us who lived and ate back then, evocative of suburbia and simpler times.

Since then, a confluence of intercultural and culinary events and inventions, enough in themselves to fill a book, have conspired to expand and elevate our palates. The results of these, for the average cook with a normal amount of pride, and for our purposes here, are twofold: (1) our own culinary standards and expectations are much higher than they used to be, and (2) so are everyone else's.

I can remember, vividly, a few culinary turning points in my own life. One was the first time I ever tasted really good Szechuan food, which appeared in New York City around the time I did, though to greater fanfare. I was stunned by it: the clarity of the flavors and textures; the spiciness; the colors of the food, so distinct and pretty. Later I realized that by tasting that meal, I was also saying good-bye to canned chow mein and the comforting if mushy meals served in old-fashioned Chinese restaurants in strip malls, none of which tasted right anymore by comparison.

Not too long after that, Italian restaurants stopped serving gloppy beige food and started serving *pasta*. Not macaroni, not spaghetti as we'd all known it, but *pasta*, concocted a million different ways, it seemed, and also cooked al dente, so that you couldn't as easily pretend, as children of my generation did (with great hilarity), that you were eating worms.

Next came fresh herbs—amazing cilantro, rosemary, basil, thyme—available even at the supermarket pretty much year-round. All these made the most ordinary food taste different, better. And then one's first taste of real Japanese food, Thai food, and now fusion food, all these cuisines and others (Cuban, Vietnamese, Yemenese!) mixed and matched every which way. Sophistication, however, exacts a cost. After tasting all this, none of us can very well go back to dousing cream of mushroom soup all over our dinners. No, if we want to eat well, we have to cook well. Which sounds like a daunting prospect, but it doesn't have to be that bad.

My motives for learning to cook were hardly unique: I learned to cook to please a man. After that, I cooked some more to please another man, and so on. Many meals and several boyfriends later, I finally got married and, by the time I did, was both thrilled and horrified to discover that I was cooking practically every night, entertaining a lot, and had somehow acquired a reputation as a Good Cook. Acquiring a reputation as a good cook, I also learned, is like earning a reputation for promiscuity: People will expect you to put out—meals, that is, in the case of the cook.

Not that I mind; I like to cook well, I certainly like to eat, and I also like being thought good at something so essential and nurturing. Yet when I watch friends of mine who are passionate or professional cooks at work in the kitchen, I know that I'm watching a different league of cook entirely. These people actually enjoy devoting a whole day to dinner, and they'll go out of their way to do things from scratch when they could more easily (and, in many cases, in my opinion, just as effectively) do those same things from a box, package, or can. They're process-oriented cooks, chefs really, who derive their pleasure from the ritual of preparing a meal. I'm more goal-oriented. I do like to cook, but only up to a point, and certainly not all day. I like presenting meals better than I like preparing them, and I welcome any shortcuts that will help speed me to the finish line—dinner.

If I don't care much about the process, I do, however, care about the results. We're short on ceremony in these microwave and take-out times, and a shared meal is a ceremony, arguably the oldest ceremony there is. If you've cooked it yourself, it's also a gift. Which is why, I think, those of us who like to cook, those of us who *think* about liking to cook, or even those of us who don't much like to cook but have to cook anyway, keep seeking out the next recipe or the latest cookbook: to keep the ceremony alive. (Which is not to say we want to keep it alive every single night and never go out and have someone else do the cooking.)

Anyone who has even a nodding acquaintance with a kitchen can make any of the recipes in this book. They're just recipes, some more exciting and some less exciting than others, but all are as close to risk-free as they can be. I've adapted many of them, often in last-minute desperation, from other, more difficult recipes, in order to stay one meal ahead of my family and friends; that good-cook reputation is not without its disadvantages. Some are original, some have been passed around a lot, some come from friends, and some are homespun versions of things I've tasted in restaurants. Basically, this is good home cooking that can be mixed and matched with extra courses to get you through any entertaining occasion as well.

Above all, each of these recipes is doable by an amateur. I know, because I am one and I've done them all, and more than once, just to be sure. On request, I've also passed along many of them to friends, with no complaints so far. I know, in fact, that because it's good, slightly different, and perfectly easy to make, my broccoli–goat cheese pasta has by word of mouth made its way around the country to friends of friends like a chain letter.

To me, a new cookbook is a success if even a few of the recipes become well splattered, well loved, and eventually committed to memory like lyrics to a familiar song. I hope you'll find at least a few of these to be worth splattering—and worth serving.

Part One

ATTITUDE: Minimum Effort, Maximum Praise

Repertoire: The Fewer Recipes the Better

I don't understand the philosophy behind dividing recipes into such categories as company meals, everyday meals, meals for special occasions, or meals that will really impress: Shouldn't whatever you cook be the same for whomever you're feeding? If your family loves your linguine with simmered Cheerios, why then isn't it good enough to serve the Smiths? Why should we have to *impress* people, anyway; isn't it enough simply to feed them well?

Lazy and less-than-confident cooks get rattled, I've noticed, by two bad habits: (1) Not trying hard enough to cook good meals when they're cooking anyway (everyday meals), thereby reinforcing the notion that they're inept, and (2) trying way too hard to cook for special occasions (company meals), thus getting tangled up proving themselves with recipes that are too complicated for any sensible person to take on. Combined, these two habits are totally self-defeating. You won't learn to cook, for one thing. For another—and even more important—you won't have any recipes and menus to see you through either ordinary nights or special occasions.

The truth is that you don't actually have to *be* a good cook to *appear* to be a good cook. All you have to do is to master a few good, easy, slightly enlightened recipes (everyday meals), recipes with a gourmet aura around them. For special occasions, take these same, already special meals (good enough for family, good enough for friends) and serve them—along with a compatible first course, to raise the meal a formality notch; a salad course, if the meal seems to call for one; and dessert. This add-a-course philosophy takes the tension out of entertaining, because the basic recipes will already be as comfortable and familiar as a worn-in pair of jeans. Having your repertoire down pat also puts some pleasure, taste, and ceremony back into hectic weeknights.

Why make a fuss on an ordinary Tuesday? Simple. Because it takes as much time and effort to make a bad meal as it does a good one. If you're going to be cooking chicken anyway, why not cook it with the specific goal of finding five or six really good, pretty easy chicken recipes that you can go back to time and again? How many more chicken recipes do you need? If you cook a proper chicken dinner once a week, with six good recipes you'll have each only once every seven weeks, which is not enough to bore your family and friends to tears, but certainly enough to qualify as a respectable chicken repertoire. Plus you can vary the things you serve with the chicken; mathematically speaking, those five or six recipes can spin off into infinite variations.

I've seen many noncooks become cooks in just this way. One friend of mine, for example, a staunch noncook, began to date a man from out-of-state, which made it easy for her to continue not cooking. Once the relationship grew serious, however, he decided to come visit her for a week: seven dinners, or, rather, six, she said, because surely they'd go out at least one night.

She had one recipe at the start, her standby dishwasher fish, in which a boned fillet of fish wrapped in tin foil gets poached throughout the course of a dishwasher cycle (no soap). All her friends faxed her their favorite menus, those that *appear* difficult to make but aren't, and she picked the ones that rang truest to her. More to the point, she *made* them, night after night for all six nights. Now that she and her out-of-stater are married, she continues to collect recipes. "Thirteen dinners, top to bottom," is her repertoire, which, mixed and matched, has seen her through three years of marriage so far. Starting from scratch, excluding dishwasher fish, she has mastered meals at the rate of four a year. And her husband thinks she's a good cook.

It's the recipes that make the cook, in other words, not the other way around. Add to those five or six chicken recipes a few gourmet-aura pastas, lamb and beef dishes, fish and pork recipes—you get the idea. Quality recipes, and only a few in each category: That's enough. Obviously, anytime another good recipe falls into your lap, you can add that to your repertoire; meanwhile, all you do is rotate the already good recipes you have in each category.

While you're rotating all your favorite meat, poultry, and fish dishes, it's just as important to rotate the side dishes, to give the illusion that a different and astonishing meal is coming out of your kitchen every time you go to the trouble of cooking.

All cooks, good and bad, and at one time or another, fall into ruts, putting blinders on against all the other possible things there are to cook: "Well, those string beans were fine last week; might as well have them again tonight." By giving in to string beans that second time, you're precluding artichokes, fennel, endive, leeks, grilled radicchio, and a host of other slightly out-of-the-way vegetables that will yield you more gourmet mileage and not take any more time or effort to make. You're also falling into a string-bean rut, a syndrome I understand, since I've often fallen into broccoli ruts myself. A leek rut would be worse still, I imagine, but leeks once in a while make for a nice change, as in, "Oh, leeks. How nice for a change." Nice changes give the illusion of good cooking. And all it means is to vary the vegetables.

Too much change too fast, on the other hand, can be bewildering to your loved ones. I once had a mild anxiety attack in the supermarket, reaching, as I do every week, for the low-salt stoned wheat thins, which my husband, Michael, consumes as snacks at the unusually high rate of a box a week. I suddenly had visions of Michael, helping to unpack the groceries and thinking: "Oh, God, low-salt stoned wheat thins, not again! My life's become so routine, my marriage so predictable. . . . I'd better run off with someone else who at least is more creative about crackers." Possibly it was true, too, that I myself was tired of buying low-salt stoned wheat thins so relentlessly.

I was relieved to have anticipated the demise of my marriage in time to save it, and that week bought several different kinds of crackers—some poppy and sesame seed things, I forget what else. As Michael unpacked them, I watched carefully for his reaction, which was "Where are the stoned wheat thins?" After a somewhat edgy week in our marriage, I went back to stoned wheat thins and our old ways, and I feel better now knowing that if he runs off with someone else, at least it won't be about crackers. People like change, but not too radically or just for its own sake.

With that in mind, what I've tried to do with the recipes in this book is to think of slightly unusual ways to make usual fare, and to put some background foods, the kind that most of us don't usually prepare because we forget about them, into the foreground for a minute, so that we'll remember them and give them their occasional due. None of the menus have to be followed recipe for recipe; if I've suggested rice and you'd rather have potatoes, by all means go ahead.

These are weeknight menus, by which I mean that if you feel like cooking a good meal after work, you'll be able to prepare and cook any of them and be ready to eat by dinnertime, long before the eleven o'clock news. They won't take all day, in other words. They're also company menus, in that they're good enough for company (good enough for family, good enough for friends). To turn them into dinner party fare, just add a first course to the beginning and dessert at the end.

Is there an overriding philosophy or influence that defines these menus? Not really, because I don't have one. Instead, I've picked, chosen, adapted them from here and there because they sounded good at first, tasted good when I made them, and are hard or nearly impossible to fail with. Some may include ingredients that cost rather more than, say, a box of Kraft macaroni and cheese, but then these are *real* dinners, homemade-from-scratch meals for when you want to sit down with family or a couple of friends, perhaps with candles, music, and a bottle of wine, to remember that the world is still a civilized—and delicious—place to be. As to whether the children will eat them, the answer is maybe yes, maybe no, the same way they take to or don't take to anything else you serve.

There are, however, a few general principles you can keep in the back of your mind to make things a little easier on yourself:

• The first trick is simply to relax. Some of the foods most popular today—pastas, risottos, Mediterranean concoctions—are essentially peasant dishes, everyday fare from their countries of origin, created with room for some error. Sometimes risotto turns out a little soupier than other times, for instance, and it doesn't matter. It tastes fine anyway. Just because a food has an exotic-sounding name and has been given a gourmet spin doesn't mean it's hard to make. Polenta is another example: It sounds intimidating. Instead, thinking of it as cornmeal mush, which is essentially what it is, makes it sound less exotic. But when you serve it, serve it as polenta.

• Fruit is hardly a culinary tip or secret, but usually when we think of fruit's place in a meal, we think of dessert. Yet insinuating fruit somewhere else into a meal is a sophisticated touch, and tasty, too; the sweetness of fruit is a good counterpoint to more somber dishes like lamb and pork. Pineapple with ham, cranberry with turkey, chutney with curried things—these are standards. But you can stretch the idea farther, particularly in the summertime, with fresh peaches or apricots buttered and grilled alongside the meat. Pineapple can also be grilled to accompany pork. Fruit salsas are relatively new to most of us, and there's one spelled out here that's really good with salmon. Also, salad with fruit is classic, and I've always felt that the more complex you make the salad, the less complex you have to make the rest of the meal.

• I think most of us worry too much over the "piping hot" issue, when we should be thinking more about room temperature. Realistically, the odds of having every person seated at the table when every dish arrives piping hot, then serving everyone the piping-hot food, then have them eat it before it stops being piping hot are slim to none. "Eat it while it's hot" is what every cook says but, in my experience, few people pay attention. The microwave helps, heated plates help, heat-retaining serving dishes help, but it's still rare to burn your tongue on anything at a seated dinner. Ways around it?

When possible, especially when entertaining, seat people at the table before bringing in the food; dawdling time will thus take place before the food arrives.

If you're carving meat or poultry before it goes to the table, it'll obviously cool off faster, which is fine. But if you're putting a sauce on it, make sure that the sauce is *very* hot and goes on at the last minute; that way, it'll warm the meat.

Try to plan menus where not every single dish needs to be piping hot. Like asparagus, for instance, many other vegetables—well-prepared string beans are a good example—can be brought to the table slightly warmed but not necessarily piping, and they'll hold up fine, particularly next to a dish that *is* piping hot, like mashed potatoes. Beets, carrots, broccoli, and sautéed squashes are other vegetables that are fine just warmed. Things like bean or lentil salads are supposed to be served at room temperature, and are also good bets.

As long as there's one steaming hot element in the meal—a cup of soup served first perhaps—main-course salads, compositions of meat or poultry with vegetables or beans spooned around them, can even be served in the winter; they're totally easy, and a great boon to entertaining.

If you're serving a one-dish meal like a pasta, take the servings from the bottom of the pot. This will keep distributing the heat—and the sauce.

• A number of the recipes in this book start with the same instructions: Sauté a shallot or two in butter or oil, add wine and chicken broth (canned, preferably Campbell's, is fine), and boil till the liquid is sludgy, reduced to between a third and a fourth of its original volume. Sometimes various other things are thrown in and reduced as well. This is known as a reduction, anyone can do it, and once you can, you can whisk any number of other things into it (gorgonzola and rosemary, dry mustard and sour cream, goat cheese and thyme . . .) for perfectly lovely pasta or meat sauces, and no one will ever know that a good percentage of your repertoire starts with the same technique. The alcohol evaporates, the stock flavor intensifies, and the shallot pierces the reduction, which acts as a vehicle—like a suitcase—to carry other flavors. Please don't skip over these recipes if you think reductions sound complicated. The reduction actually happens pretty much by itself, it's easy, and the technique will see you through many a meal.

• As a general rule, creative marinades (in my humble opinion, but also that of scientists) are a waste of time; in most cases, oil, vinegar, salt, and pepper work as well as any more complicated concoction you dream up. A marinade is designed to soften the connective tissue, not flavor it, and the vinegar (or lemon juice or wine—the acidic part of the marinade) is what does the trick, while the oil gives body to the acid. As for flavoring (which is what people hope for when they add all kinds of other stuff to a marinade), it's easier to flavor the meat or fish by brushing them with a flavored sauce just as it's at the point of doneness. To take a common example, chicken to be grilled outdoors is often soaked in a barbecue-sauce–type marinade, with ginger, soy sauce, ketchupy things, whatever, then put on a grill. What happens? It burns. Barbecue-type sauces have sugar in them, and what you want is acid, to soften that tissue. Marinate instead in oil and vinegar, then brush your sauce on at the very end. The chicken won't be blackened to smithereens this way. Marinate at room temperature; it works faster. The most economical way to do it is to put the meat into a plastic bag, secure the open end tightly around the meat, and turn it over as often as you think of it. This way, you can get away with using less oil, which is expensive.

• Enlist the help of a butcher. Not for ground round, or boneless chicken breasts or standard fare, but for the times you want the meat in effect to sing. Most of us were raised in the days of supermarkets, when butchers were hidden away behind soundproof plates of glass. Even today, many of them will come out, if you ask them. Independent butchers, too, are still around, and I've never found a friendlier or more helpful lot. Take medallions of pork, for instance, which you probably won't find precut in the supermarket. Tell a butcher what you want, on the other hand, and he'll cut you perfect medallions from the loin, and even pound them, if you ask. Or costly veal chops, admittedly a splurge. In my experience, they're not very good when bought over the counter, and why splurge on something that's going to be a disappointment? But I've never had a bad veal chop from a butcher and, again, he'll pound them for you if you ask. (Pounding meat yourself, by the way, isn't very hard, either.) Or duck breasts. Who thinks of cooking duck breasts? Hardly anyone. They're easy, though, they don't have to be fatty, and most butchers keep a supply of them frozen back in their mysterious closets. All you have to do is ask.

I've just read that a woman may reduce her risk of a stroke by 68 percent simply by eating a carrot each day, and do a number of other good things for herself besides. Scary, compelling, and weird, fun facts such as this turn up all the time now in the news, inspiring us to do things like buy (and eat) extra carrots for a week or two before going back to our lackadaisical a-carrot-here, a-carrot-there consumption. Like it or not, most of us are creatures of habit, and many of our habits are pretty dismal at that.

Still, all the new information about eating to ward off cancer, heart attacks, cataracts, and just about everything else is sobering; when you're cooking for people you love, presumably you'd just as soon keep them healthy, not to mention alive. But how? There's *so* much information to process, that to get it right—and, at the same time, make it palatable—seems just about impossible. If you add up all the things we're advised to eat all the time (or never), it's confusing at best; at worst, it makes you want to sit down with a bag of Chee-tos and call it a day.

I once had a friend watch in horror as I put a whole stick of unsalted butter into a big pot; you would have thought I'd just stirred in a hand grenade. I was making risotto, an Italian rice dish. "But a whole stick of butter!" she exclaimed. Well, yes. This was risotto for ten, and neither margarine, which I wouldn't have used anyway, nor olive oil would have done. There were plenty of other wholesome things going into it—onion, skinless chicken breast, chicken broth (homemade, as it happened), mushrooms, parsley (which is, surprisingly, not just a throwaway garnish but has anticancer properties, among salubrious others), the rice itself. In fact, the butter-per-guest quotient, expecially given that the risotto, along with fresh bread, was the main course, seemed to me fine, even restrained. Preceded by a seafood and white bean saladlike concoction and followed by a green salad and a light dessert, the meal felt satisfying and balanced, and I didn't feel one iota of guilt about the butter.

I'm an amateur cook, not a nutritionist, but I do know that by cooking well at home, you can pay closer attention to what you eat (and don't eat) than you can by letting someone else decide how much butter goes into the risotto. As a perennial weight watcher, I know, too, that if I eat truly pleasing meals—which is to say the kind that meet not only the FDA's daily requirements but also sometimes include the tiniest bit of the supposedly forbidden—it's easier for me to keep my weight on track, at least with a little help from the Stairmaster. My secret suspicion is that health-fanatic gram counters use up years of their lives with worry and stress, and that the occasional bacon cheeseburger can lift the spirits enough to undo the damage it might cause otherwise.

Scientists are discovering as if for the first time what ordinary, sensible people have known all along: that you are pretty much what you eat. Anyone who cooks, or anyone who eats, will be fascinated by the new books on the healing and preventive properties of food—nutri- ŏr foodaceuticals, as they're starting to be called. (I've listed a couple of these books here, in the Notes on Sources.) These books—and once you start reading them, they're as addictive as a good mystery—popularize recent studies linking health, sickness, longevity, and diet. On the one hand, what they demonstrate won't shock you: Most of the things you already know are good for you are in fact good for you, and most other things aren't. But there are also a few surprises in these studies: Curry, ginger, cloves, cinnamon, mustard, honey, and a host of other things we don't think about too much one way or another play a significant role in our well-being.

The best thing about reading these nutritional tracts is not learning how enzymes, minerals, antioxidants, and phytochemicals work, because you'll read this part, say to yourself, "How interesting!" and forget all you've read by dinner. The best part instead is looking at the lists of foods and their beneficial properties. Not that you'll necessarily remember all these, either, but the good foods will stay in your head like a mantra, and you'll find yourself seeking out ways to add, say, a red pepper, or turmeric, cantaloupe, bananas, or cauliflower to more of your meals.

Still, man cannot live on turmeric alone and, as a cook, I do use some butter, in risotto and elsewhere, and a few other red-flag ingredients (like half-and-half and heavy cream) can almost always be found in my refrigerator. Why would I keep heavy cream, if I care about nutrition? Because I also care about taste, and sometimes just a smidgen, literally, of heavy cream or half-and-half whisked into an ordinary sauce, nutritious or not, can smooth it out and improve it enough to make it, for me, worth the risk of a raid by the nutrition patrol. And if the food tastes good enough, you won't go sneaking off later to eat something much worse than a percentage of a smidgen of heavy cream. "Aim high, but settle for moderation" is not, I suppose, the most disciplined or health-affirming motto there is, but it might well be the most life-affirming.

Ultimately, I can't help but resent the notion of foodaceuticals or nutriceuticals: Can't we just call a food a food? It's bad enough that nobody goes out anymore for a nice bike ride on a pretty day; now it's all about helmets, stretchy tights, and how fast you can pedal to get your heart rate up. Highways now have information on them, not people traveling to quaint places. I wish we could at least leave food alone, not tart it up with clinical-sounding names. It's useful, I suppose, to know that oysters on the half shell are full of iron that helps produce hemoglobin, and also zinc, but aren't they more fun to eat because they're romantic, extravagant, and slurpy? (And easy to make. Don't be embarrassed to ask a reputable fishmonger to shuck the oysters for you—everyone does; they're really hard to shuck on your own. It's also worth trying to cajole him into giving you some seaweed on which to serve them, but crushed ice or chilled plates will set them off almost as well. Serve with Tabasco sauce, which has been found to kill any bacteria that might be lurking in raw shellfish. And eat them right from the shell.)

The Japanese have a traditional axiom that says it's wise to eat thirty different things a day, which sounds like a lot—but think about it. Cereal, milk, banana, juice, coffee, a few oysters, and a carrot:

That's seven right there. The Japanese were notoriously healthy until they started adopting a few of our eating habits, and this axiom suggests that variety and moderation will keep body and soul intact and sated; you can't eat too much of any one thing, good or bad, if you have twenty-nine others to go.

Denial inspires excess, I've always found, not that I mean to set myself up as a model, just as one example. I used to be of the I-never-keep-any-sweets-in-the-house school of thought, and the approach always worked fine, for a few days, until I thought I might do some serious damage unless I had a cookie RIGHT THEN. So I'd rush out to buy (and eat) rather more cookies than I should have, before going back to never-keeping-any-sweets-in-the-house. Then one breakthrough day I bought cookies when I didn't even feel like eating cookies. It was a great comfort somehow just to *have* them there, not unlike keeping a thermometer or Band-Aids in the medicine cabinet . . . just in case. And now I always have cookies in my cookie jar. I've certainly eaten to excess since then, and I've certainly eaten cookies since then, but I don't believe I've actually eaten *cookies* to excess since then.

You won't find it in books on nutriceuticals, but you will find in the Bible a note about using food to nourish the soul as well as the body (Ecclesiastes 8:15, Revised Standard Version): "And I commend enjoyment, for man has no good thing under the sun but to eat, and drink, and enjoy himself, for this will go with him in his toil through the days of life which God gives him under the sun."

I think this means that, like everything else, the nutriceuticals should also be taken in moderation.

Presentation: When What You See Enhances What You Get

Presentation, presentation, presentation is to the realm of cooking what location, location, location is to real estate: practically everything, or at least a good part of the battle. Many recipes add a note at the end telling you to garnish with parsley or watercress or any number of things, but if the plate is too jumbled or crowded or chaotic by then, a sprinkling of minced parsley or a sprig of watercress is just going to make it look worse. By envisioning how the plates will look before you cook a thing, on the other hand, you're halfway there. Even if something goes wrong with the execution, at least the meal will *look* okay.

Michael and I once went to a dinner party on a Saturday night where the menu was cheese straws as an hors d'oeuvre; sliced chicken breast, sautéed and prettily sliced, with white rice and steamed sugar snap peas as the main course; a tossed salad; a slice of chocolate tart. Afterward we went out and each had a slice of pizza with onions and mushrooms, served on flimsy paper plates, with an ice-cold beer right out of the can.

What was missing from that chicken dinner was love, energy, spice, taste, color—any kind of a touch that marked it as special. Sautéed onion tossed in the rice; chopped parsley, a glaze of wine and the pan juices (perhaps with a few capers and a lemon wedge) for the chicken; fruit, a wedge of cheese, and a fresh hot loaf of bread with the salad: All of these would have helped. Any single *one* of these would have helped, would have given the meal depth, texture, zest, energy, *life*. When you enter a room, your eye searches out the corners, the colors, the possibilities inherent therein. Your eye does the same thing when confronted with a dinner plate, as does every other one of your senses—even that of hearing, which is drawn subtly to the crunch potential. A mix of colors, tastes, textures, smells always improves the look and therefore the taste of a meal.

Our unadorned, predominantly white meal, served as it happened on white plates, was wholesome enough, it's true, but such a letdown, after we'd gotten all dressed up and everything. The bubbly pizza, however, in the clattery pizza parlor, felt just right, presentation and all, the way each meal in its own way should feel.

This is not to suggest that anyone spend hours carving up radishes into curlicue shapes, arrange the food into have-a-nice-day smiley faces, or burn the tips of your hair trying to flambé something en route to the table. Just try to make the whole thing look pretty.

Tried and true garnishes like parsley, watercress, and lemon wedges or slices are fine, sure, but look around to see if you can find something else from time to time. The variety of herbs available all year long helps presentation and taste and, in the summer, you can also use edible blossoms like those from chives or nasturtiums on top of salads or to garnish a plate. A shaving of ginger, if the dish has an oriental feel to it. Serving mussels or clams? Use the shells as garnish. Instead of a lemon wedge, try a slice or wedge of an orange, if the dish would taste good with a sweeter fruit. Instead of a plain white napkin, wrap hot bread in a clean, bright plaid kitchen towel. If the meal is plain old hamburgers, put all the condiments together in a basket. If the meal is all white, chop some red pepper from a jar onto something in it, along with some parsley. If the meal is all red, would a couple of black olives fit in somewhere? (If the meal is all brown, you've made the wrong meal.) Good cooks also always wipe the edges of plates and platters with a paper towel so that the plates don't look haphazard. None of these take much effort, but they all seem as if they do.

Then there's the two-plate trick, which also falls under the heading of presentation. The question to ask yourself is this: Which of the dishes going onto the dinner plate would be better set off on a plate of its own? Boneless breast of chicken, mashed potatoes, and asparagus is a fine dinner, for example, just as it is, but when all the ingredients are smooshed together on a plate, it looks like diner food. Food needs breathing room, and plates are easier to arrange prettily when they're not heavily weighted; a groaning board is, when you think about it, a pretty unattractive concept. Asparagus is often served as a first course in fine restaurants: Why not present it that way at home? Or at least on a separate plate?

Another culinary tactic that's taken me a long way is what I think of as creative layering and which means, basically, that a food with something served under it and something served over it looks (and tastes) more important than a food served all by itself.

Take that same breast of chicken and serving of mashed potatoes above, where you've moved the asparagus off the plate entirely, leaving you with an all white dinner. You can layer it in as many ways as you can think of, thereby giving it more taste, color, and texture, an illusion of complexity—without going to very much trouble. How?

- With a slice of tomato peeking out from under the chicken, and a drizzle of store-bought pesto on top;
- With an underpinning of thin-sliced sautéed (just until they wilt) onion and fennel, and sprigs of fennel on top;
- With a slice of baked eggplant on the bottom and a drizzle of store-bought tomato or marinara sauce (with fresh basil snipped in or not) on top;
- With a few sprigs of watercress peeking out one end and a spoonful of cranberry relish with crumbled walnuts and a little more watercress chopped into it at the other end;
- With a piece of toasted Tuscan or peasant bread on the bottom, and mushroom sauce (see page 88) on top;
- Or skip the asparagus and serve the chicken on a bed of Swiss chard or spinach, with a drizzle of butter and parsley or chives on top;

- Or skip the mashed potatoes, put the asparagus back on the same plate, and serve the chicken over pureed canned beans or artichoke hearts—same drizzle of butter and parsley or chives on top;
  - And so on. Toasted pine nuts, other nuts crumbled or chopped up, leftover spoonsful of pasta sauce, store-bought salsas, bits of cheeses . . . Not that you'll necessarily want to spend too much time thinking about it, but the possibilities are endless.

Making a big deal out of a salad is another presentation trick. By elevating the salad to a separate course, as the French do by serving it after the entree, you give yourself lots of leeway for ways to vary it, and to make the entire meal seem grander. While you wouldn't dress a salad up with fruit or cheese (or both) if you were serving it with the main course, as a separate course these additions give a meal a gourmet cast. Crumbled Gorgonzola, baked goat cheese, slivers of fresh Parmesan (shave them with a vegetable peeler), for example—all these make a simple tossed salad seem like something more (and take no time and very little effort). Sliced pears or apples, a bunch of grapes, fresh blueberries with watercress: Again—no time, little effort, and the meal feels special.

You can also use the salad to round out what seems missing in the rest of the meal. Say you're serving a vegetarian main course, and feel you want to infuse the meal with just a touch of meat. Doesn't have to be in the main course at all; just make an arugula salad with a slice of prosciutto and a Portobello mushroom (see page 108) for everyone you're serving, and the meal will have a little of everything. Or elevate the salad still another notch to make it the meal itself. Room-temperature composed salads are among the easiest meals to prepare, very sophisticated in feel, and great for entertaining.

Presentation, then, doesn't have to be still another cooking chore, but a kind of culinary sleight of hand that can, without adding anything to your actual cooking time, seduce the people you're feeding into thinking that you've gone to a lot more trouble than you have. Take that same chicken, mashed potato, and asparagus dinner, add to it a salad, and watch it gain stature as it represents itself. First course is now the asparagus, served on a plate by itself, very pretty—maybe with a little minced parsley on top. Entree is now the chicken, with a slice of tomato underneath and a drizzle of store-bought pesto on top, with the mashed-potato accompaniment—also pretty, tastier, and no extra trouble. Then comes the salad course, a tossed green salad, but with a narrow wedge of good cheese and a small cluster of grapes on each plate. Doesn't it feel like a more splendid dinner? With very little extra effort?

It sounds cynical, perhaps, to compare the preparation of a family meal to a value-added marketing scheme, but then I wasn't the one to invent the "nothin' says lovin' like something from the oven" concept. That's a haunting jingle, with so many dinners behind us and so many more still waiting to be made. Anyway, these are cynical times; even when resources and energy levels are low, expectations remain high. Clever packaging matters in the marketplace. Why not let it work to your advantage in the kitchen?

Entertaining:
Countdown to an Easy Dinner Party

I love the *idea* of entertaining, which usually occurs to me a week or two ahead of the actual *fact* of entertaining. The idea inspires visions of a candlelit table covered in a crisp linen tablecloth, the glitter of polished silver, a perfectly cooked dinner arranged just so on elegant plates, scintillating debate and sparkling conversation among company dressed in costumes from an Edith Wharton novel.

The appointed day arrives, and now I'm dreading the whole thing; I've left out of my vision several reality-based elements. The shopping ordeal, for one. Or that I might have invited someone who can't eat what I feel like cooking. That my candlesticks are all covered in wax from the last dinner party, because it grew hot and someone opened the outside door, which blew wax all over the place. That my crisp tablecloth is actually a limp old blue thing, also covered in dripped wax, with a few miscellaneous stains besides. That my flatware is not silver at all, but mismatched stainless steel. (No elegant plates, either, and only eight that match, while ten people are coming—no, twelve people! The X's just called to say they have houseguests; is it okay to bring them? Why did we invite the X's, anyway?) And nobody I know (except Y, who always overdresses, to make the rest of us look horrible) dresses for the dinner parties of dreams.

Funny ritual, the dinner party, isn't it?

Still, I give dinners a lot (Y has more outfits than anyone has a right to), at least in part because I have the routine down pat enough so that it's no longer anxiety-provoking. My favorite moment every time is just before the guests are due when the table is set (homey, if not the resplendent table of fantasy), I'm freshly showered and dressed, we've just put on music, the house looks as sparkly as it's ever going to, and anything can happen. I like, too, the moment of anticipation when everyone is seated and I'm about to bring in the first course. By the time the main course has been served, assuming everything's turned out okay, I stop worrying. We're past the big hurdles. Even if the rest of the meal (salad, dessert) goes awry, at least no one will starve.

Every host has his or her own routines and favorite ways of doing things. Some people use the opportunity of entertaining to pull out all the stops, cooking the hardest things they can think of and working themselves and their kitchens into, as it were, a stew. Some people lie about whether the coffee is caffeinated or decaf when they serve it. My own favorite ways of doing things involve making the evening to come as easy for me as possible, without causing too much distress to my guests.

I try, for example, never to stretch out a dinner party—shopping, cooking, serving, eating, cleaning up—into more than a day's work and, if possible, to execute the whole thing in even less time. Menus that suggest that the sorbet course can be prepared three weeks ahead don't interest me very much. I've found, too, that cooking a good meal for twelve doesn't take any more time, really, than cooking for six, so if you're giving a dinner party reluctantly, you might as well shoot for a full house. One dinner party, one day (or less): That's long enough for me.

Make sure the culinary centerpiece to your meal is available before you shop for the odds and ends that go along with it. That is, if you're planning to serve crab cakes, get your hands on the crab first, before buying all the other stuff that goes into crab cakes.

Doing the countdown backward, giving yourself a little extra time (for mishaps, phone calls, bad hair day, etc.) for each step will tell you how long the meal should take. If the guests are coming at seven-thirty, start there and, once the shopping is done, begin subtracting.

If setting the table takes twenty minutes, round up and subtract half an hour—you're down to a seven o'clock starting time. Subtracting half an hour to make a twenty-minute dessert brings the starting time to six-thirty. Half an hour to make the salad and dressing, six o'clock; half an hour to dress—five-thirty. An hour, give or take, for the first course and the main course: now four-thirty is the starting time. Allowing half an hour for cleaning up the mess you've made so far, and making sure that you start the dinner party with the dishwasher empty, brings your starting time to four.

So you start at four, which isn't so bad, really; rushing's worse. The object is to have everything feel serene by seven-thirty. You might like to be doing something in the kitchen when your guests arrive, so they won't think the meal has been catered, but it's better if you're not in your bathrobe, with a stricken look on your face, holding a frozen turkey.

To save time and energy with the meal itself, first of all skip the hors d'oeuvres.

If your dinner guests are invited to come at seven-thirty, they'll know that dinner will be served at about eight, eight-fifteen. If you go to the effort of making elaborate hors d'oeuvres, either the guests—most of whom will be dieting anyway—will ignore them to feel virtuous, which will be annoying, or they'll eat them all and dull their appetite for the meal itself. What is more, if there are elaborate hors d'oeuvres all over the place, people will eat them casually (and uncomfortably, since it's always hard to eat elaborate hors d'oeuvres without spilling) and not notice them enough; rarely has anyone remembered how terrific the hors d'oeuvres were if he's eaten an entire meal afterward. And for some reason, platters of hors d'oeuvres set out in the living room are always the last things cleaned up, which is depressing.

Aim for suspense instead. Put out a bowl of Pepperidge Farm goldfish—or black olives, drained cocktail onions, peanuts in their shells, carrot sticks: some little edible distraction. And serve dinner, beginning with a fairly substantial first course, on time.

Maybe I'm projecting the way I feel onto others, but I've always thought that guests are most comfortable once they're seated in their places. The candles are lit, they know who they're supposed to talk to, they know they're going to be fed soon, and they know that they can go home after that.

By bringing in an elegant first course at just that moment (or, if it's not a hot dish, by having it already on the table as the guests are sitting down), you set the pace of the meal—leisurely—and the tone: The food should be taken seriously.

A well-planned first course also reduces the cost of a dinner party by a lot.

When I plan meals, I always do a rough calculation as I go along of the CPP: the cost per person. The rule is to allow about half a pound of meat or fish per person, but it's a rule highly dependent on what else you're serving along *with* the meat or fish. If you've served a first-course–sized portion of pasta, for instance, the way the Italians do, you can literally reduce the amount—and cost—of the meat or fish you serve by half, to a quarter of a pound per person. If your first course is a salad-related affair, you save yourself the trouble of a salad course. The first course is also a good opportunity to fill in any elements—fruit, cheese, various textures—missing from the rest of the meal you've planned.

First courses also buy you time in the kitchen before you have to come up with the main course. Your guests aren't hungry anymore, and you can clear the plates and load them into the preemptied dishwasher while they're sitting in their places and not getting in your way. (I always do a sweep at this time, too, and load the cocktail glasses and the Pepperidge Farm goldfish bowl into the dishwasher, tidying up course by course, so to speak.)

The dinner party is now at its partly-sated-but-still-anticipatory stage, and you actually have twenty or twenty-five minutes to clean up, warm the main-course stuff already in pots, warm the dinner plates (I admit I usually don't, but it's a classic touch), spoon the dinner onto platters, and just generally deal with things before the natives get restless. As the main course goes onto the table, you can also load the pots and pans and miscellaneous spoons and bowls into the dishwasher—and run it. On the quick cycle, the clean dishes will be ready to put away at the same time the entree is finished, you'll have an empty dishwasher to accommodate the dishes from the main course and the salad, if there is one; in addition, sometimes the still-warm first course dishes can go right back onto the table for dessert. Phew. When this clean-as-you-go method goes according to plan, you'll have only a few odds and ends to clear up after the guests leave, and just time enough before you go to bed to talk about Y's new outfit.

Having just read through one dinner party, perhaps you don't want to think about another just yet. However, if you truly hate to entertain and owe more people dinner than you care to think about, the easiest way is to have two dinner parties back to back. Make a double portion of the first course and a double portion of the dessert the first day, and you're practically home free for the second party, particularly if the tablecloth is clean enough to make it through one more night.

Part Two

THE COOK'S ARSENAL: Stalking the Stores

The Supermarket:
Scanning the Shelves for Shortcuts

The way my husband, Michael, and I have divided up the household labor, I do most of it, including the cooking—and also the shopping, no mean feat, as any shopper knows. To date it's just the two of us, plus two dogs who'll eat most anything, but since we both work at home, shopping has to cover breakfast and lunch virtually every day, official and unofficial snacks, and dinner more nights than not. This means one major trip to the supermarket every week, plus forays every day or two to specialty stores, perhaps for fresh bread, fish, fresh vegetables, or whatever else we've run out of.

Cooking from meal to meal or dinner to dinner is a far cry from cooking just here and there, I've learned. It's more work, for one thing. It's also more challenging, because you have to figure out things like how to segue a few leftover string beans into some other meal, and what to do with the rest of the cardamom you bought specifically for a recipe you thought might be nice but which everyone hated. There's nutrition to consider, along with variety, balancing the diet, ingredient availability, and how long things take to make compared with how much time, not to mention energy, you have at the moment. It's not easy.

I've also learned that cooking starts with shopping, because the more creative the shopper, the more creative the cook.

Fearing or loathing the supermarket is a big mistake, because the supermarket, if you pay attention, will be your ally, an endless source of shortcuts and ideas. Trouble is, most of us do the shopping so by rote—the milk's here, tea's over there—that we miss the culinary possibilities in between. It's often been said, too, that we tend to shop at eye level, looking neither too far up nor down: If, in other words, you were a foot shorter or taller, you'd buy entirely different kinds of cookies, jams, and mustard. Might be fun to explore a shorter or taller person's cupboards to see what you're missing.

Diet books will tell you never to go to the supermarket when you're feeling hungry, a sensible point. Even so, don't go right after a big meal, when you're feeling sluggish and depressed, because if you do, you'll buy only low-fat cottage cheese, which means you'll have to turn around and come back the next day, by which time you'll probably be feeling hungry again. Go when you feel like cooking, and you're likelier to find something good to cook.

Or shop with a friend who cooks.

I once made a date to meet a friend I hadn't seen in a while at the supermarket one night at ten o'clock, which turned out to be an oddly intimate way to catch up. It started badly. Upon entering the store with our carts, she automatically headed right, toward the frozen foods, while I veered left as usual, toward the bread. "But the frozen stuff will melt," I said. "No, it won't," she insisted. "Anyway, who wants to put a bunch of frozen stuff on top of all the fresh stuff?" We agreed that I'd go her way this time, she mine the next.

I was glad I did, because seeing the supermarket through someone else's eyes can teach you a few things.

In the frozen food aisle, for instance, her first stop was in front of the burritos. I had never even *noticed* frozen burritos, much less tasted them. But she and her husband both work at home, too, and frozen burritos, she pointed out, can be made in four minutes in the microwave, served with bottled salsa, low-fat sour cream, and sliced fresh avocado, eaten in about two minutes, and can pass for a fine lunch. Selective sampling of convenience foods can expand your repertoire by a lot, and variety is certainly as good a spice as curry. In that same aisle, for some reason near the frozen waffles, was a small rack of Pepperidge Farm soups; she recommended the vichyssoise, and she was right.

In the next aisle—cranberry juice, which is big at my house. Every morning we mix a little cranberry juice with orange juice (freshly squeezed as a treat on the weekends), one quarter cranberry juice, approximately, to orange juice. Orange-berry, is what a friend's daughter, who likes its pink color, calls it. Somehow the cranberry juice seems to cut the acidy sensation of the orange juice. Technically, this doesn't make sense, because cranberry juice is itself acidic, but it works anyway. With a summer lunch, you can do cranberry-orange with seltzer and (optional) a squeeze of lime. Or, for a special occasion, cranberry-orange with champagne. Or cranberry-grapefruit, which you can buy premixed, but it's better and cheaper to make your own. In short, we go through a lot of cranberry juice. That day, however, my friend reached up to the top shelf above the name brands and pulled down the supermarket's own brand of low-calorie cranberry juice. So did I, and never went back.

I copied her as well when she put a jar of sliced pickled fresh ginger, which I'd never noticed there by the prunes, into her cart. Fresh ginger, of course, is a terrific knobby thing, but you have to use it up pretty fast or it dries up and gets puckery, and you have to be a far better chopper than I am to get those wonderfully thin slices that accompany sushi in Japanese restaurants. But if you happen to keep a jar of it around (Sushi Chef is the best brand I've found), there are millions of ways to use it—as a garnish on grilled tuna or chicken and vegetables, a curl of it atop my mashed potatoes and eggplant, to sweeten sautéed red cabbage and apples, a twist of it on sorbets, etc. It's the kind of thing you don't know you're missing until you have it lying around, and now I always do.

I know for a fact that my friend discovered veal and turkey sausages that night for the first time, because she asked about them when I put them in my cart before she put some into her cart, too. Long and thin like hot dogs, not squat like Italian sausages, and sold around here under the brand name Schaller & Weber, these sausages are stocked in my supermarket rather mysteriously by the pesto, not by any of the other sausages. Grilled, or sautéed in the tiniest bit of olive oil, they get a nice dark brown stripe on each side once they're cooked, they're light and really tasty particularly served with honey-mustard sauce, my version of which (see page 178) is the easiest one I know, for lunch or a light supper, served hot, at room temperature, cold, doesn't matter. Grown-ups also like them on hot-dog rolls, with mustard and red pickle relish.

And I gave her my pancake trick.

I was once invited to a three-star restaurant and ordered as a first course blinis, crepes, pancakes, or whatever you want to call them, topped with sour cream, smoked salmon, and salmon roe. The blinis, which tasted much more "gourmet" than any pancakes I'd ever tried before, had dill in them, I remember, and were delicious. As for smoked salmon, any occasion with smoked salmon in it is all right with me.

I figured the dish couldn't be all that hard to replicate, but when I started looking up pancake recipes, each of which had at least ten ingredients, I thought, "Well, maybe not." Years went by. Then for some reason I paused one day in the pancake department at the supermarket, and there was a row of Maple Grove Farms of Vermont pancake mixes, including one for honey buckwheat pancakes. (In gourmet stores, too, I've since noticed other brands of fancy pancakes.)

I made the mix, snipping fresh dill into the batter and putting the box away before my guests came. (I always tell the truth when asked, but why advertise?) Separate little bowls and plates set out prettily on a tray held smoked salmon (each slice cut into three our four smaller slices—they'll go farther that way), sour cream ("lite" sour cream works fine), chopped Bermuda (red) onion, lemon wedges, and more dill, for garnish. That first time I also included a tin of salmon roe on the tray, with a *very* small spoon to suggest the appropriate portion size, to which no one, including me, paid attention. When the guests came, I did the pancakes (an egg ring or tuna can open on both ends makes them perfectly round), put two on each person's plate, and let the guests compose their own first course.

The variations are endless: Keep the roe and omit the salmon or vice versa; substitute (cheaper, though not quite as good) golden domestic caviar; vary the theme entirely by offering smoked blue-fish, trout, or even canned smoked oysters with chives, instead of dill, chopped hard-boiled egg, and a creamy horseradish sauce; and so on. Anyway, people love them, they're elegant as can be—and they're *easy*. Really easy. I make them a lot and each time I do, I shudder to think that I might never have paused at the pancake mixes on that fateful day.*

We were silent, my friend and I, when we got to the canned beans, for we both know that canned beans can be put to thousands of uses in the kitchen; we just loaded up on Goya, all shapes and sizes. In my excitement, though, I came home that night with two cans of hominy instead of the chick-peas I'd meant to buy, and eventually I had to do something with them.

---

*One complaint and warning, though, and this doesn't apply strictly to Maple Grove Farms pancake mixes; there are many, many other culprits. In each box there's enough for one batch and then some, but not quite enough for two batches, so you have to keep buying more of it in order to use it up, if you see what I mean. I hate that.

Hominy? I've tasted grits, of course, but not being Southern, I had no idea what hominy was, other than something to do with corn, or what to do with it.

The Joy of Cooking, always a good place to start, offered a recipe for hominy cakes, in effect a corn version of potato pancakes. The kernels, however, which seemed even as I was mixing them too big to form cakes, were in fact too big to form cakes and so didn't stick together: We ended up with what looked and tasted more like hominy hash browns. Even so, the corn taste came through nicely. A Southern friend came up with a simpler way: Drain them, pulse briefly in a food processor so that the kernels won't roll all over the plates, heat them up, and serve with butter, salt, pepper, and finely snipped chives. Some people, too, add the tiniest bit of cream, and I admit I'm one of them. In any case, they're a refreshing from-time-to-time alternative to potatoes or rice (or kasha, couscous, etc., for that matter) and, unless you're serving a tableful of Southerners, your guests (Europeans especially) will think you're very clever to have thought of hominy.

Bagging at our adjacent checkout counters, I learned something else about my friend. The game I always play at the checkout counter is Beat the Cash Register, whereby I try to get everything into bags any which way before the checkout clerk totals the bill. It's not a very imaginative game, I never win, and it leaves me with many bags too heavy and some too light, but I like it. My friend, on the other hand, bags more sensibly, each bag filled with things that go more or less in the same place—cleaning equipment in one bag; frozen foods in another; produce in a bag all its own. She also has a young son, who has his own kitchen cupboard, below the counter so he can reach it, where he keeps his cereal, snacks, favorite bowl, and a few toy soldiers.

And he unpacks his own bag each time, excellent training for a young boy, even in these supposedly gender-enlightened times.

It's also a good idea to explore other supermarkets and gourmet shops than your usual haunts; loyalty is virtuous and all that, but blind loyalty to one food shop can cause you to miss out on all the quirks, specialties, and bargains that make some customers loyal to all those *other* food shops. When you consider the exorbitant price of good olive oil, for example, you'll also consider where best to buy it.

There are two supermarkets to speak of (and one that's unspeakable) near me, and usually I go, as I did that night with my friend, to the one that's bigger and brightly lit, with aisles that make you want to roller-skate. I like it, too, because sometimes there are volunteers outside, collecting food for the needy and homeless. They'll give you a list of the items they need most, and you can buy them right there and donate them on your way out. Supermarket number two, on the other hand, is sleepier and doesn't have much in the way of fresh produce. But it has generic dried mushrooms for about a dollar an ounce, it always has duck, it has lemon curd. And it has me as a customer, about once a month.

Dried mushrooms—shiitakes, chanterelles, porcini, morels, etc.—are as gourmety as can be, and there are a million different ways to use them, except that in general they're too expensive to toss into things willy-nilly. These generic dried mushrooms, however, whatever they are, work just as well as any of the fancier ones (except maybe morels) and, at that cost, you *can* just toss them into things with relative abandon. As for duck, it's just as easy to roast a duck as it is to roast a chicken, once you know how, and which sounds more exotic to you? Lemon curd, though hardly an everyday item, is not only good for various dessert purposes and to serve with bakery-bought scones but it's also a crucial ingredient for lemon curd chicken breasts, and is one of those things to have around that in general make people think you know what you're doing, even if your tart is made with frozen puff pastry.

(Which is sold at the other supermarket.)

When I was much younger, I once fell in love with a man because he used kosher salt. In his kitchen—this man loved to cook—he had, next to an enviable industrial Garland stove, a small blue crock with a lid, always filled with kosher salt. There were also copper pots and other kitcheny things hanging everywhere, every cooking gizmo you can imagine, a fireplace, and a reading chair in that kitchen; it seemed like the coziest place in the world. When he was cooking, instead of sprinkling salt from a shaker, as I'd always seen it done, he sprinkled it with his fingers. Because grains of kosher salt are irregular and bigger than those of processed seasalt or the iodized salt you "pour," you can really feel the friction in your fingers as you're sprinkling once you get the hang of it, which takes only about two seconds. And if you wash your hands in kosher salt after playing around with garlic or onion, the smell will go away.

Salt has a long and noble history (the word "salary," for instance, comes from the Latin word for salt, because Roman soldiers received a portion of their paychecks in salt), and it's only in our time that we've grown klutzy with it, oversalting everything in sight so that doctors tell us to cut down on salt, etc., etc. However, salt is essential to life and to cooking well, and by using it judiciously, you'll discourage people from oversalting their food at the table, which is one way we get in trouble in the first place.

Anyway, I feel immensely cheered when I go to someone's house for the first time and see the salt in a bowl instead of a shaker; to me, it's a sign that the person is a real cook or at least is going to give the meal an enthusiastic try. Not that kosher salt isn't sometimes pesky. When it's humid, it absorbs water like a sponge, but then salt is *supposed* to absorb water: Iodized salt is actually covered with a chemical (not harmful) to keep the grains apart. If you learn to put salt in by feel, as you do with kosher salt, you're less likely to get distracted and make mistakes.

Where you don't want salt is in your butter; good cooks use unsalted (also called sweet) butter when they use butter to cook with. The salt in butter is put in mainly as a preservative, but in the whole time I've been alive, I've never once run into rancid butter, salted or otherwise, and probably neither have you; moreover, most of the butter we come across is so processed against rancidity as to make the salt virtually redundant. Even worse, "lightly salted" means different things to different butter-makers and, since consumers like salt, they may well salt with a heavier hand than one would like, though I haven't tasted enough salted butter to know for sure. If you need a final argument, try this: Butter not watched carefully can burn, and salted butter burns sooner than unsalted, so if you forget you have longer to remember in time.

A good cook's kitchen is a mysterious, seductive place, and everytime I'm in one, I poke around as much as the cook will let me. Most cooks are generous about sharing what they know, and you can learn a lot along the way about what you're supposed to do with this item or that. Not always. Once I visited a cook who had a good-size jar of juniper berries set among his bottles of oil, vinegar, and the like. "What are they for?" I asked. "My port wine sauce," he said, but that's as far as he'd go. So while I think it would be extremely chic to be able to rattle off five inventive, clever, and easy things to do with something as unusual as juniper berries, I really don't know that many. I do, however, often see them listed as ingredients for pork recipes, and a few tossed over a pork chop never hurt anybody.

One gourmet might shudder at another gourmet's pantry, of course—these are subjective matters—but here, in no particular order are some staples I would never have thought of stocking in any regular way before I learned to cook. I've often watched other cooks use them, or sometimes happened upon them myself, and a couple of the shorter entries are so obvious as to be banal. In themselves these items won't necessarily turn anyone into a better cook, but some of them will help immensely in accessorizing a meal or giving a bland dish some zip. Real gourmet or faux, you'll use these staples if they're *there*—and become a better cook in the process.

Oniony Things

Scallions, shallots, red onions, Spanish onions, fresh garlic . . . this may seem like a lot to have around at the same time, but if you do keep them around, they all make cooking a lot easier.

Scallions (also called green onions) are those long oniony things that come tied with rubber bands, and are the easiest way to flavor a salad. Just chop them, green part and all, and throw them in. They also can be chopped into cream cheese to flavor it, or grilled or broiled (brushed with oil) whole, as a little added attraction edging a plate.

Shallots look like little onions and are in fact sold near the onions, and sometimes have a nice purple tint at the edge when you peel them. The flavor is that of a concentrated onion. (Unlike other oniony things, you'd never eat them raw.) When in doubt, a shallot chopped fine and sautéed can enhance a lot of things—paillard of chicken or veal, even a simple piece of sole or flounder, and provides the flavoring for many intense reductions.

Red (sometimes called Bermuda) *onions and Spanish onions*. Red onions are most often eaten raw (in salads, etc.); when used in cooking, they're used for their color as well as their flavor. Spanish onions are those with a slight yellow tint (as opposed to the onions known simply as onions, which are the ones that really make you cry when you chop them), are slightly sweet, and the all-around onion to use for soups and sauces; sometimes they're eaten raw as well.

Garlic. How can you pass for a cook unless you always have fresh garlic around?

Tomatoy Things

Culinarily speaking, high tomato season has to be the best time of the year, when vine-ripened tomatoes can feel literally warm from the sun as you eat them—plain, as if they were apples; rubbed on toasted bread with garlic and olive oil; in bacon, lettuce, and tomato sandwiches; tossed into cooked pasta with fresh basil, black olives, and maybe some cheese; worked daily into salads any which way. . . .

The rest of the year is low tomato season, when recipes still call for tomatoes, but the ones in the supermarket look pallid and feel like tennis balls. What do you do then?

Canned (whole peeled) *tomatoes* are nothing to be ashamed of using, and they turn up as ingredients in cookbooks far more ambitious than this one. Surveys I've seen say that the best ones—less acidic and don't taste like cans—are Italian.

Tomato paste. Any recipe calling for tomato paste usually calls for only a tablespoon or so, which is why tomato paste in a tube makes much more sense than that in a can: Who wants to open a can just to use a little bit? Sun-dried tomato paste has a little more gumption and can be substituted anytime.

Plum tomatoes. If you want or need fresh tomatoes out of high season, plum tomatoes, if you can find some that yield to the touch, are a pretty good bet, even for salads.

Things to Chop Up and Sprinkle onto Other Things for Color, Flavor, Texture

Capers. Not the little mingy ones that look as if you forgot to grind the peppercorns, but the big fat ones (by caper standards), big enough to chop up or flamboyant enough to throw onto anything you've first sautéed with shallots. Really good cooks, at least the ones I know, always use the fat capers. They're a great garnish for any number of salads—seafood salads, bean salads, salads with almost anything unusual in them. Even a tuna salad, made with canned tuna, hard-boiled eggs, carrot, red onion, and parsley ground up in the food processor with a bit of Hellmann's mayonnaise to bind it, served open-faced on fresh toasted peasant bread with capers on top, can turn an ordinary tuna sandwich into one that's better, even if your kids would probably rather have it the usual way.

Black olives. My personal favorites are the wrinkled ones known as Moroccan olives, which often have been marinated in rosemary and a little oil, and which will last a long time in the fridge. If you don't keep them around they won't occur to you much, but if you do stock them as a staple, they can garnish anything capers can, including many salads, and then some. They also belong in a number of pasta sauces, they're great with egg dishes, compatible with fish, chicken, veal, and some fish dishes, and are standard fare served in a bowl as an hors d'oeuvre or with supper-type meals like sausages, new potatoes, a salad, bread, and a big wedge of cheese. Fresh or bottled are fine. Forget the ones in a can.

Marinated red peppers. Pimentos are fine for some things but too limp for others, and when I discovered big jars of cut-up red peppers, pickled with the skin still on, in the supermarket, I began to discover, too, various ways to use them. The marinade is on the sweet-tart side, and a pleasant trace of it remains when you blot them with paper towels. They're absolutely terrific on sandwiches, for one thing. Imagine a simple turkey sandwich on whole-wheat with lettuce. Now imagine it with a slice of crispy marinated red pepper as well: It really gives the sandwich a whole new dimension. Minced, too, for numerous salads, or chopped up (with capers, olives, and parsley) to dress swordfish, chicken, or veal, it adds texture, a little extra bonus of taste—and color; red is lovely on a plate. Plus you can reuse the pickling marinade, by slicing cucumber or fennel with onion (or whatever), dropping the new vegetables into the jar, and waiting for just a day to enjoy a perfectly fine homemade accompaniment to whatever it seems to go with. (This sounds like a Suzy Homemaker tip but it really works; the marinade can go on, tasting better with whatever you add to it, probably for years.)

Fresh (or bottled) ginger, lemon peel, orange peel, fresh herbs, bits of tomato or bacon or meat or sausage, last night's vegetables, hard-boiled eggs, sun-dried tomatoes . . .

Oils and Vinegars

Cooking oils. Cold-pressed extra virgin olive oil is the best, if you can afford it (try a price club or gourmet warehouse for well-priced olive oil). Also good to have around is plain old vegetable oil, which does the job while imparting virtually no odor. In many dishes, half butter and half vegetable oil will give you a full butter taste with a higher burning point; in other dishes, you need oil but don't want it to impart a specific taste, the way olive oil does.

Flavoring oils. Hot chili sesame oil, which comes in little bottles and is available in most supermarkets, imparts a spicy, exotic edge, sort of oriental in feel, to various foods, and is also a great thing to have around. A dash of it improves almost anything stir-fried, particularly jumbo shrimps or prawns, and it's also good in salads and marinades. While hardly staples, new, intense flavoring oils—orange, lemon, truffle, herbal—are finding their way into gourmet markets; you use just a few drops diluted with oil or butter to distribute the flavor to meats, vegetables, grains, or pasta. They're expensive (white truffle oil especially, a few bottles of which would send your kids to summer camp, which might be a better investment; black truffle oil is cheaper), but they go a long way. Recently I was called upon to make lunch for four, and all I had was a bunch of leftover microwaved broccoli. So I cooked a pound of pasta, tossed it with maybe half a teaspoon of lemon oil, a little butter and vegetable oil, and the broccoli: It was actually quite delicious. I've served lemon-oil fish and lemon-oil pasta (with parsley, no broccoli) as a side dish ever since I splurged on a bottle of it not long ago (five ounces for fifteen dollars, cheaper than a good perfume at least), and I still have two thirds of the bottle left, which makes the cost seem less extravagant. It's certainly easy to work with and, if you care to cast fiscal prudence to the wind, you'll probably get more compliments on it than you would on five ounces of Chanel No. 5. As with the Chanel, just a few drops (literally) at a time.

Vinegars. Several kinds if possible, including balsamic (still the best, I think, for many things, including simple green salads), red and white wine vinegar (so as to be able to make different kinds of dressings), and Champagne vinegar, for elegant occasions. Champagne vinegar has a sparkly flavor—you can almost imagine bubbles—and its clarity seems to make certain salads, like seafood salads, practically float. I also keep plain old Heinz white vinegar around, to make this really good cole slaw with no mayonnaise (see page 125) or fruit salsas to serve on top of simply cooked fish.

Condiments

Mustards. Honey mustard, Colman's dry mustard, any Dijon mustard, and any other mustard you want. You can subtly vary the taste of vinaigrettes just by varying the mustard, which is one reason to keep several on hand. Plus mustard has any number of other uses—mixed with oils and herbs to glaze meat or fish; whisked into a creamy mustard sauce (see page 178); just as it is on sandwiches and hamburgers; to flavor lunch salads (e.g., egg salad).

Chutneys, premade gourmet relishes, store-bought salsas, various pickled things. In supermarkets and gourmet shops, there are now dozens of good things to eat in jars, so why not eat them? Someone recently brought me a jar of cranberry nut conserve, for example, and I thought, "Oh, great, what am I going to do with this?" In fact, I used a spoonful to garnish chicken breasts one night, another spoonful with turkey sandwiches one day, another spoonful with sliced loin of pork—and the jar was gone, months from Thanksgiving. Same with salsas: If you think about what goes with what, you can always come up with something. Tomato salsas are great with fried eggs, for one thing, and you don't need butter; you can fry them in vegetable oil and serve on a heated-up store-bought tortilla and make huevos rancheros right at home. Instead of bread and butter pickles, try pickled cauliflower, eggplant, or watermelon rinds—just for a change. As for chutney, it's great with any curry-related dish, somber meats like certain cuts of beef, and even on sandwiches.

Jalapeño pepper jelly. Sold at most gourmet shops and some supermarkets, jalapeño pepper jelly is, well, jelly made from jalapeño peppers. It's transparent jelly and, as you'd expect, spicy. A spoonful of it is terrific with meat loaf, and it's good spread on a sandwich (meat-loaf sandwiches especially, and honey-glazed chicken or turkey). At a friend's house I also once had a truly extraordinary, shiny brown sauce on veal chops, and when I asked my friend what it was, he said it was jalapeño jelly melted into homemade reduced veal stock. In my "lab" I fiendishly tried to find an easier way, and have re-created his sauce rather well, I think, without homemade reduced veal stock. It's also good on lamb chops, pork chops, and eaten right from the pan with a spoon. Visits to farmers' markets and gourmet shops can yield other surprises in the jelly-jam department, so look carefully. A friend who often visits us for weekends once arrived with a jar of rosemary-garlic jelly, for example. Hard as it was to imagine it on top of an English muffin, it was easy enough to imagine a teaspoon of it on top of a pork or lamb chop, melted just as the chops are finishing their broil.

Flavor Intensifiers

Canned chicken stock, for the 90 percent of the time you don't happen to have any homemade on hand. I used to use a brand that shall remain nameless but now I use Campbell's Hearty Request. A food writer in a newspaper I read recently did a survey of the best canned stock and chose Campbell's. She was right.

Chicken Bovril, or concentrated chicken stock. Foul-tasting on its own, Bovril can help to intensify a chicken-related sauce or soup, especially if you remember to shake it well. I probably shouldn't admit this, but I also use Bovril to jump-start homemade stocks. Many chicken stock recipes, for example, call for four pounds of chicken bones. Now if you've just cooked a chicken that weighs only five or six pounds before it's eaten, where are you going to find those extra pounds of chicken bones? You're not. Nor are you going to do anything like freeze the chicken bones you have until you get some more. Probably you'll throw them away. Or else you'll follow my recipe, which is to put the bones of at least 1 chicken in a stockpot, with 1 chopped-up onion, 2 chopped celery stalks, 2 carrots, 2 bay leaves, some fresh parsley, and a handful of peppercorns. Fill with water to the point where you can still see an inch of chicken bones showing (there won't be enough bones to justify any more water), add 1 tablespoon Bovril (it's hard to remember but you're supposed to shake it first), bring to a boil, reduce the heat, and simmer for an hour. Strain it, chill it, and remove the fat that rises to the top with a spoon. You'll end up with perfectly okay stock if a little less of it than four pounds of bones would yield. You could also use beef Bovril for beef stock, but Kitchen Bouquet browning and seasoning sauce is really better. It smooths out a meat sauce and does pretty much what it promises it will on the label. You can also add a little of it to a sauce you've reduced with chicken stock and turn the sauce glazy and brown, if that's the color you want.

Old Bay Seasoning. I guess it's the "bay" in the name, but I always associate this with—and use it for—seasoning seafood, which it does really well; it's said also to be good for chicken, meat, etc., but I've never tried it on anything other than seafood. You can mix it into flour or bread crumbs when you're sautéing a piece of flounder or deep-frying calamari, or you can sprinkle it on the fish directly.

It's good, and the tin it comes in looks as if it has looked the same way for a century, which is always nice.

Probably a few other things you don't normally keep on hand will turn up in the recipes themselves, but I thought this was enough excitement for now.

The Inevitable Note About Equipment

on't you hate it when cookbooks tell you essentially to throw away all your kitchen equipment and start anew, or else you'll never learn to cook? This is nonsense; most classic recipes were developed when people were still grinding their own flour and cooking outdoors because they had to. Considering the present mismatched state of my own kitchen equipment, for me to make any such suggestions would not only be the pot calling the kettle black but would also be a futile gesture, because why should you? I know that if I have a little extra money lying around, I'd much rather spend it on a sweater than a boning knife, Henckels or not.

Still, every cook has a few odd and favorite things that he or she thinks indispensable. I know a woman who whenever she goes anywhere takes her stovetop percolating coffeepot with her, a beat-up old thing that looks as if it should be used on a campfire, and I know someone else, a man who cooks very well, who is so deeply attached to his copper pots that he won't let anyone else touch or polish them, much to his wife's relief.

I've been known to travel with my *mandoline,* so named because the motion of slicing with it is much like playing the instrument itself, except that you can do it even if you're tone deaf, and potatoes and things come out at the end, not music. Despite the lyrical name, it's nothing more than a vegetable slicer, and I think it's my favorite kitchen gadget.

Perhaps a mandoline is not tops on every cook's list of necessary items, but once you have one you may well add it to yours: For me, it's indispensable. The old ones are wooden and handsome, worthy of hanging on a kitchen wall. I have a new-fangled version, easier to use and clean afterwards, plastic (and under twenty dollars at good kitchen stores). With it doing most of the work, you can actually (and without much trouble) make potato chips, shoestring potatoes, and a nifty potato tart, all of which will make people think you're a splendid cook regardless of how the meat turns out. You can slice a cucumber perfectly evenly in a matter of seconds; apples and pears; onions and fennel (for my onion and fennel salad); cabbage, root vegetables, and so on. You can also live without one and slice these things very carefully yourself, or you can skip over recipes that call for the use of a mandoline, though you'll miss some good things that way.

Nor could I do without my simple potato ricer, the poor cook's food mill and still—after all these years and culinary advances—the best and simplest way to make proper mashed potatoes: Boil the potatoes unpeeled, nudge them through the ricer (the peel comes right off), and whip them vigorously as you add the butter, cream, or whatever you want—they can be garlicky, oniony, etc. And you can make purees galore starting with the ricer: celery root and potato; pear or apple and potato; parsnips or turnips with any of the above, any of which can get you through an autumn or winter dinner party with gourmet aplomb. They cost about four dollars.

Other Equipment I'm Attached To

The blender, for all kinds of soups and some sauces, including strawberry sauce, the basis for myriad desserts.

The food processor, for chopping, grinding, pulverizing.

The microwave oven, for cooking many vegetables (and popcorn!), melting, defrosting, heating, or reheating. Largely with the help of Barbara Kafka's breakthrough *Microwave Gourmet,* I'm making my way into microwave cookery but still find most things easier to do on the stovetop. Also, learning to use a microwave before learning to cook on a stove is like learning to use a calculator without first learning how to add, subtract, multiply, and divide for yourself: You have to understand a process thoroughly before switching to its shortcuts, particularly a process like cooking, which relies on all the senses. When a microwave really shortens the cooking time or improves the recipe, it can be a thrilling accessory in the kitchen. But even with a microwave, you can't turn a dinner that conventionally takes an hour to make into a three-minute triumph. Alas.

Good all-purpose kitchen shears. When I'm cooking in other people's kitchens and ask where the scissors are, I'm often amazed when they go off to the bedroom or the office to find them: How can one not keep scissors in the kitchen? A professional chef, I know, can pulverize herbs into tiny little bits by going back and forth over them really fast with a chef's knife or a mezzaluna (two sharp half-moon arcs with handles on top, very official looking), but I can't—or I could, I suppose, but it would take forever. It's either because I'm left-handed or clumsy, but I've never mastered fast, neat chopping, much as I admire it. With shears, all you do is snip the herbs and they come out just fine. They're also handy for cutting open food that comes in plastic bags; cutting the string on roast chicken and other poultry; snipping ends off string beans; and cutting out recipes you're never going to make. And keep a sheet of sandpaper somewhere near the scissors; by cutting it up mindlessly (a good thing to do when you're on the phone), you'll sharpen the scissors. As for poultry shears, my butcher has very nice ones, thank you.

CONFESSION: Even in these low-fat times, I love my deep-fryer. I may be dead wrong about this, but deep-frying at home seems like not the worst thing to do to your guests from time to time, for special occasions. One of the great cooking mysteries to me is that when I deep-fry something—

homemade potato chips or calamari rings, for instance—I end up with almost exactly as much vegetable oil as I started with, even after I've blotted whatever I've fried on cut-up pieces of paper bags. (I know this, because you have to strain the oil back into its original bottle, so that you can use it again.) This unsolved mystery has emboldened me to keep deep-frying just once in a while, and you can do it too (It's surprisingly easy), if not with an actual deep-fryer then with a big solid pot and one of those hand-held Chinese stir-fry strainers.

Optional but nice is an *ice-cream maker*, not a big electric one necessarily, but one you keep in the freezer; they're available for about thirty or forty dollars. And you don't even have to go to all the trouble of making ice cream: Sorbets are a wonderful gourmet flourish, and all they require is pouring some juice into the ice-cream maker, turning it occasionally, and serving in a creative way. Like beet sorbet (I kid you not) served over warmed goat cheese with dressed cabbage. Or a sweetened citrus fruit sorbet (grapefruit, orange, lemon, or lime) with bits of rind in it, served as a light dessert with sweetened ricotta. Or bottled guava juice, peach nectar . . . you get the idea.

Pots and Pans

A pot, for the record, has two handles, one on each side, while a pan has one long handle. As a general rule, pots and pans need to have some heft to them in order to distribute heat well and thus cook the food evenly, without burning it. As a more specific rule, whatever pots you already like are probably the best ones for you to cook with. There's a lot of snobbism in the world of pots and pans. Don't fall for it. If your beat-up Teflon pan set, circa 1972, has seen you through ever since, that's all you need to know.

When you see the enviable-looking and expensive chef's sets of pots and pans offered in department stores and cooking catalogues, what you're paying for is heft (and brand name and advertising, etc.), and heft comes in a variety of terrifically functional-looking styles, the best of which work well and look extravagant, even sexy, as pots and pans go. James Beard advised against buying a whole set, because you'll end up paying for a size you'll rarely use, but if any expensive pots and pans ever come your way, grab them.

Most of us, however, probably make do with mismatched cookware, and end up using the same few pots and pans more often than anything else. I confess to a couple of Teflon pans I like, and I also have a few good copper pans, which I received here and there as gifts; they make me feel I'm in France every time I use them. They're heavenly to cook with and classic as well to use as serving dishes. There are downsides, however. Copper is lined with tin (or stainless steel, nickel, or silver) and sooner or later (later, in most cases, unless you burn something early—but still) you'll have to find someone to reline the pot once the copper begins to show through, which might not be easy. Also, copper absolutely has to be kept polished to a brilliant sheen or it loses its magic, and keeping it gleaming is a considerable chore. I'd happily do it, however, were I given more such lavish gifts.

Wish lists aside, I also have two chef-level pans (a fry pan and a saucepan) and one good-size pot, and I use these more than anything else. For the pots, you can get useful plastic handles to cover the metal ones, which over time will save you many burned fingers. You probably already have a Dutch oven without knowing it—it is nothing more than a big, often enameled casserole with a lid; Creuset is one familiar brand name. I've never actually heard a Dutch oven called a Dutch oven in polite company. I also have a big stockpot, which I use for stock, cooking pasta, and the like. It's a cheap one, though, which I regret, because things are always sticking to the bottom.

I have an overly fastidious friend whose attitude toward cast-iron skillets drives me crazy: "But they never seem *clean*." That's ridiculous; of course they're clean, in a cast-iron-skillet kind of way. They're not expensive, and they're fine things to behold, once they're all blackened and broken in. (If seasoning them sounds like an arcane ritual, it isn't. Cast iron is porous, and seasoning it—swishing vegetable oil all around and baking it at 300 degrees F for an hour, then wiping out the oil—evens the surface.) The smooth surface requires only soap and water, no scouring, and the very slight filminess that remains signals not that the pan is dirty but that it's ready for use.

For cooking at high heat, cast iron is superb. Say you have a nice piece of swordfish, which you want to cook in your cast-iron skillet. Heat the skillet till it's hot enough to make you nervous about it, sprinkle a teaspoon of kosher salt in the pan, then throw in the swordfish. Turn it over right away to seal the first side that meets the heat, then turn it back over again at once; both sides will be sealed. Turn the heat down to medium to assuage your nervousness (the pot will remain as hot as it needs to be), and cook for no more than three or four minutes per side, depending on how thick the fish is; cut into it once or twice to make sure it's just cooked through. You'll have delicious, juicy blackened swordfish, which you can serve with a sauce if you want, a drizzle of butter and lemon, or just plain. Light a few candles, too, because the kitchen will smell kind of fishy, and lit candles help clear a room of odors. It'll be worth it.

Knives

Knives are another complicated subject, with a long history that begins with cavemen and -women and isn't over yet.

One confusing factor is that when you begin to read about knives, you'll learn that the best knives have blades made either of carbon steel or stainless steel, in particular high-carbon stainless steel. Technically this is true, but nearly all knives sold today, or anyway ones any of us might buy, are stainless steel. Carbon steel is fine, but the blades discolor when set against half the things you might want to cut up, so it's yielded the market to stainless steel. If you happen to see a fine-looking knife at a yard sale or antiques store, though, don't pass it over just because it looks tarnished. You've probably got a good buy on your hands, and to clean it up all you have to do is rub some scouring powder onto it with a cork. The cost of stainless steel knives varies, obviously, with their quality; better knives are weighted better, forged better, attached to their handles better, that kind of thing. Better knives are a pleasure to use, and if someone gives you a set, or even one such knife, you will have received a marvelous gift. If not, you'll probably muddle along with the knives you already have, which is fine. Let's hope, however, that you have enough versatile knives to get most jobs done, and that you go to the trouble of sharpening them once in a while, because the difference between a sharpened knife and an unsharpened one is dramatic.

Besides a paring knife, a big chef's knife, and the various intermediate knives you already have, a bread knife, and it doesn't have to be an expensive one, is a really nice thing to have.

There's such wonderful fresh bread around now, much more so than when I was a kid, and any meal is enhanced with a loaf of it—daily bread. It's a shame to hack it up with a knife that will leave the cut end flattened, or reduce a whole slice of bread to the equivalent of a child's rolled-up bread ball. Sure, with a baguette you can twist or break off a piece and avert the problem entirely, but not with a loaf of peasant bread or Tuscan bread, with which one makes bruschetta in all its varieties and the recipe for which would demand a bread knife so that the slices would be relatively neat and uniform.

Basic recipe: Toast or grill a slice of such bread, rub a garlic clove and brush some olive oil over it, then brown under a broiler for a few seconds to sizzle garlic and oil into the bread. Top with any of a number of salad-related concoctions—squeezed juice and pulp from a very fresh tomato with a little chopped fresh basil; chopped tomato and minced, sautéed squid with parsley and red pepper flakes; roasted and peeled peppers of varying colors; canned tuna, canned small white beans, hard-boiled egg, scallions, fresh mint in a light vinaigrette. . . . This exalted Italian sandwich makes a perfect summer lunch (can't you just picture golden filtered sunlight?) or first course year-round. But you need a bread knife.

Yard sales and "junque" shops are a good source for odds and ends of kitchen equipment—whisks, ice-cream scoops in odd shapes, mousse molds, wooden spoons. It's worth pouncing on these items when you find them, since you never know when you might want to cook something wild and risky. Once I bought two serrated knives at a yard sale, not very good ones, but I've used them ever since for chopping vegetables, because I find them more comfortable than paring knives.

Another time, I found, for a quarter, what I think is a chestnut knife, which I've never used but am happy to have on hand. That time, too, I found an odd-looking set of two ribbed interlocking ladles clasped together, which I figured out were the tool used to make those fried bird's nests (of noodles or potatoes) you get in Chinese restaurants, with some dish or other spooned inside. Since no one else I know has one, people often ask about it when they see it hanging on my pot rack. It's pretty to look at and, needless to say, most people are impressed enough to find someone with such an arcane utensil lying around that they don't even think to ask how often I use it.

Part Three

THIRTY MENUS

The sage gives this pasta dish fragrance as well as taste, the spicy sausage gives it its kick, and never once have I served it to a guest who cooks without being asked for the recipe—and I've served it a lot, believe me. In many cases, parsley is optional, but here it's essential; without it, the sauce looks rather unappealing and with it it looks fine. There's a flurry of food processing at the beginning, and otherwise not much to it.

Crunchy, more fattening than many salads, and with a sweet-sour dressing, Tropica Salad is a home version of the house salad served at a restaurant in New York called Tropica. You can organize the salad and make the dressing while the pasta sauce is simmering, and still have some time left over. This salad is meant to be served as a separate course, before or after the pasta, whichever. I prefer after.

Because spicy Italian sausages happen to come in packages of eight at my supermarket, I always make a double batch of this sauce so as to use up the whole package; it's no more trouble to make, and the sauce freezes really well. This

Menu

serves four

Penne with Chicken and Spicy Sausage Sauce Infused with Sage

Tropica Salad

Bread, if you want

way, rather than finding four pathetic sausages in plastic wrap in the freezer six months hence, I'll find instead a frozen vat of sauce in plenty of time to serve it again.

For the pasta

Tiny bit of olive oil
4 spicy (hot) Italian sausages
1 pound ground chicken
1 big red onion, skinned and quartered
1 big carrot, or two if they're small
1 cup white wine
One to two 10½-ounce cans chicken broth
½ to ¾ tablespoon ground sage
Freshly ground pepper, to taste
Penne or other short pasta such as rigatoni or radiatore; 1 pound will serve 4
Curly parsley, chopped
Grated Parmesan cheese, to serve on the side at the table

In the tiny bit of olive oil, just enough to coat the bottom of a big pan so the sausages won't stick, brown the sausages and cook them all the way through, poking the casings with abandon to release the fat. Remove them from the pan to a strainer, drain off any fat or oil around them, then put them into the food processor.

Dump out all but enough oil to cover the bottom of the pan again and set about browning the chicken. (You could do the sausage and chicken in the microwave, but in this case, actually browning them in a bit of oil gives them more texture.)

Now pulse the sausage in the food processor until it's ground to the texture of the chicken, which is to say the texture of hamburger. (You could, of course, have removed the casings from the sausage before cooking them but this way is much easier and you have to get the food processor dirty anyway, to chop the onions and carrots.)

By this time the chicken will be cooked or nearly so. When it is, pour out any extra liquid or fat that remains, trying not to pour out the chicken at the same time.

Put the sausage back into the pan with the chicken.

Now pulse the onion in the food processor, till it's also the texture of the chicken. Put it into the pan with the chicken and sausage.

Peel the carrot (or at least wash and brush vigorously with a vegetable brush, if you have one), chop into four or five pieces, and process until it's the texture of hamburger like everything else, then put it into the pan, too, and stir the whole thing up.

Add the wine, 1 can chicken broth, and the sage, and bring the sauce to a boil.

Reduce the heat to a simmer or light bubble and, with the pan either uncovered or partway covered (doesn't matter), simmer, stirring once in a while, until the whole house smells pleasantly musky, about 45 minutes. You want the liquid to boil away, but not for the sauce to dry out; it should end up moist, certainly, but not soupy. Add part or all of the second can of broth as necessary. Taste it toward the end, and add some ground pepper to taste.

Sometime toward the end of all this, put water on to boil for the penne, and cook according to the directions on the package. (If you serve pasta in bowls, one trick is to ladle some of the boiling pasta water into the bowls to warm them once the pasta is nearly done, then pour out the water just when it's time to serve the pasta.) Once it is cooked and drained, put the pasta in the bowls, ladle on the sauce, and sprinkle generously with chopped parsley. And don't forget to put the cheese, and warmed-up bread if you're having it, on the table.

For the salad dressing

Put all the ingredients in a blender or food processor and blend until they're blended.

½ cup white vinegar
¼ cup sugar
1 tablespoon paprika
½ teaspoon dry mustard
Pinch of salt
A few grinds of pepper
½ cup vegetable oil
1 teaspoon minced onion
   (you can steal a little from
   the pasta sauce)

For the salad itself

Boston lettuce (2 heads, depending on their size, will serve 4), leaves rinsed and dried
1 red pepper, sliced into thin julienne strips
1 Granny Smith apple, cored and sliced (at the last minute, to avoid browning) into really thin slices
Crumbled blue cheese, not too much, about 1 tablespoon per person
Honey-roasted cashews, whole, and not too many of them (5 per person, give or take)
Sesame seeds, about a teaspoon per person
Chives

Put the lettuce into a salad bowl, along with the red pepper strips and apple slices, and toss this much of the salad with the dressing just before serving. *After* it's tossed, sprinkle on the blue cheese, cashews, and sesame seeds. (So that the cheese and nuts won't be dressing-drenched, and the sesame seeds won't clump together.) Give another light toss. Drop the chives as if they were pick-up sticks over the whole salad, and serve. Any leftover dressing will keep in the refrigerator for a good long time.

Add-a-Course Notes

First course: Bruschetta with Red, Yellow, and Green Peppers, page 175.

Dessert: Suzanne's Honeyed Cheese, page 188.

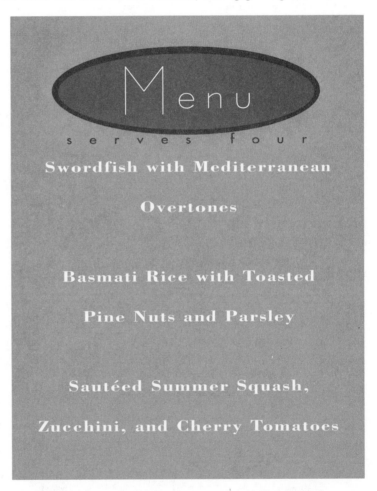

his simple—and dramatic-looking—topping for swordfish is easily multiplied (or divided) to serve as many (or as few) as you need. We have this a lot in the summer, during grilling season, when fresh swordfish is easy to come by. In the winter, swordfish is more expensive, so it's a rarer treat—but I pull the recipe for the sauce out all the time. It's just as good on chicken, veal, tuna, squashes, eggplant, and especially cauliflower; this topping on cauliflower belongs on a separate plate and can stand as a course all its own.

Tossing rice with toasted pine nuts and parsley is not a recipe to change your life, but it adds color and crunch; crumbled pecans would work, too. Squashes can be cooked all kinds of ways, but cooking them very gently so that the raw taste disappears but they never get browned is a particularly delicate way to present them.

Menu

serves four

Swordfish with Mediterranean Overtones

Basmati Rice with Toasted Pine Nuts and Parsley

Sautéed Summer Squash, Zucchini, and Cherry Tomatoes

Here, the yellow of the summer squash and the red of the cherry tomatoes are pretty together on a plate, and this dish is also a good way to get rid of all the extra zucchini that seems to pile up at the end of summer every year.

For the swordfish topping

2 shallots, chopped pretty fine

4 tablespoons olive oil

4 tablespoons finely chopped parsley, preferably curly

4 tablespoons finely chopped red pepper (from a jar is fine)

4 tablespoons big fat capers, drained and chopped

4 tablespoons chopped, pitted black olives, preferably Moroccan

Four, six, eighty—you can serve any number of people with this topping: Just remember half a shallot and 1 tablespoon of everything else per person.

Sauté the shallots in the olive oil until lightly browned. Remove from the heat and stir in everything else. Serve warm or at room temperature but not hot.

For the swordfish

½ to 2 pounds swordfish steaks, depending on estimated appetites*

Olive oil

Balsamic vinegar

Freshly ground pepper

Put the swordfish into a plastic bag with just enough oil to cover both sides, 2 or 3 dashes vinegar, and a generous amount of freshly ground pepper. Tie the bag tightly, and turn over from time to time until you're ready to cook it. Even a few minutes is enough; swordfish is very tender to begin with, and this method simply softens and oils it so that it's ready for the grill or broiler. (You don't need any herbs, either, since the sauce is full of flavor.)

Tuna or salmon, for example, can be a little rare or pinkish in the middle, but not swordfish: It has to cook through, but only *just* through. Cooking times will vary, depending on how big the swordfish steaks are and how thick, but turn after 3 minutes, and cut into the middle after another 3. When the pink stripe in the middle turns white, they're ready.

*If you serve swordfish this way with a proper first course, you can serve smaller portions of swordfish—1 to 1¼ pounds should do it.

For the rice

Follow the directions on the box for the rice itself. Chop the parsley fine. Toast the pine nuts in a toaster oven, or sauté in a small skillet (no oil needed) until lightly browned—they'll begin to smell like popcorn. Mix the nuts and parsley together with the cooked rice, adding butter if you like, along with a few grindings of pepper.

Basmati rice
4 teaspoons chopped parsley
4 teaspoons pine nuts
Butter (optional)
Freshly ground pepper

For the sautéed vegetables

Slice the zucchini and squash thickly, and quarter each slice. On very low heat, take the edge off the chopped garlic without letting it brown by warming it in the vegetable oil for about 3 or 4 minutes. Without raising the heat, add the zucchini and squash, warming that too, and stirring frequently, for 6 or 7 minutes, or until it's heated through and tenderized, and the raw taste is gone. Now add the cherry tomatoes, and warm for a minute or two, until the tomatoes are heated through but before they begin to pucker or explode. Sprinkle lightly with salt and pepper, and serve.

1 big zucchini
1 big summer squash (they're the yellow ones)
2 cloves garlic, finely chopped
2 tablespoons vegetable oil
4 or 5 cherry tomatoes per person, or more—doesn't really matter
Salt and freshly ground pepper to taste

Add-a-Course Notes

First course: Ham Mousse with Melon, page 170.

Dessert: Mix-and-Match Strawberry Sauce, page 193, or Sweetened Ricotta and Mixed Fruit, page 191.

I used to find flank steak one baffling subject (what exactly *is* flank steak? What does it have to do with London broil? What does it have to do with London? Why do you have to cut it sideways?), which is why I kept away from it for years. This turned out to be a grave mistake, because flank steak, dealt with properly, is actually delicious, even elegant, and definitely easy to make. This is one cut of meat that really benefits from an intricate marinade, although the glaze here isn't very hard to make. Flank steak is also great the next day, tender in a sandwich or served as a salad on a bed of greens and whatever else is around.

After a fair amount of research, I believe I've answered the questions: (1) Flank steak is a perfectly fine thing to cook and eat, and cheaper than certain other cuts of beef; (2) London broil is *supposed* to be flank steak, but since it's not an official name of a part of a cow, most supermarkets put the London broil label on round steak, which is an inferior cut of meat, not flank steak per se at all; (3) you have to

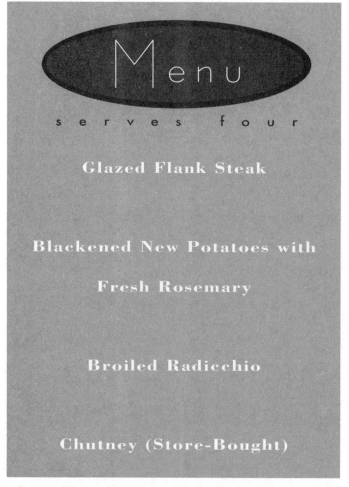

Menu

serves four

Glazed Flank Steak

Blackened New Potatoes with Fresh Rosemary

Broiled Radicchio

Chutney (Store-Bought)

cut it not sideways but on the bias, which follows the grain, and it will be not only tender but, with the slices fanned out on a plate, attractive to present. This is much easier to do with a piece of flank steak before you than it is to contemplate while reading about it.

The only other thing to know about flank steak is that it has to be served rare or at most medium rare, never well done. This is not a matter of opinion but of fact; cooking beyond medium rare clenches its muscles and toughens the meat. So it has to be cooked for a short time only, and at very high heat.

Sautéing new potatoes in this rather odd way, in the tiniest bit of olive oil also over very high heat, seems, implausibly enough, to draw the oil—and the rosemary, which is meant to char, too—into the potatoes themselves, making them moist and almost creamy inside so that they don't need butter; with their charred, crispy skin, they're good enough to eat unadorned.

Radicchio took the country by storm a while back ("What's this weird red lettuce in my salad?"), but I never really liked it much until the first (actually, the only) time I went to Venice. There, and no doubt elsewhere throughout Italy, the radicchio is shaped differently from ours—longer leaves, actual stems, heads more oblong than round—but the taste is still unmistakable. Except that Italians don't use it in salads: They grill or sometimes sauté it until it's blackened or at least browned, and the subtly charred taste is terrific.

The chutney may seem a curious addition to the meal, but its piquant sweetness clears the palate as you go along, counteracting the somber, charred (but still pleasing) note of the other dishes and pulling the whole meal together somehow. You could instead broil pitted fresh peach or apricot halves, with the barest sprinkle of brown sugar and a dot of butter.

For the steak and glaze

¼ cup balsamic vinegar
¼ cup olive oil
1 tablespoon ketchup
1 tablespoon A.1. sauce
1 tablespoon Worcester-
shire sauce
1¼ pounds flank steak
Freshly ground pepper

Whisk the vinegar, oil, ketchup, A.1. sauce, and Worcestershire together. Rub the flank steak first with freshly ground pepper, then douse the steak on both sides in about two thirds of the glaze. (The rest will be brushed on the steak, half on each side, as it's cooking.) The steak should sit in the glaze for about half an hour, while you're making everything else.

Toward the end, when it comes time to broil the flank steak, heat up the broiler until it's thoroughly hot, and put the steak under it, broiling 3 minutes on the first side and brushing with half the remaining glaze before turning. Turn, and brush the rest of the glaze over the uncooked side. Slice into the center of the steak (which, contrary to myth, won't dry out the meat) after another 2 minutes to see how it's coming; it shouldn't take more than 3 minutes on the second side, 4 maximum, for rare meat. Again, don't cook flank steak beyond medium rare or you'll be sorry.

For the potatoes

Olive oil
2 dozen new potatoes
(the small ones),
approximately
2 tablespoons fresh
rosemary, snipped

Coat the bottom of a big heavy pan or skillet—one with a tight-fitting cover—with a skimpy amount of olive oil, just enough so that there are no bare spots. Rinse the potatoes, shake off any excess water but don't dry them, and put them into the pan along with the fresh rosemary, which you have snipped off the stems.

Turn the heat to high, cover, and do nothing until you begin to hear alarming sizzling noises, then turn down the heat, wait for a minute (so as to reduce the chance of being splattered), and look into the pan. When the skins of the potatoes have blackened on the bottom, put the lid back on and shake the pan vigorously, as if you were making popcorn the old-fashioned way. Turn the heat back up to medium and repeat, shaking the pan vigorously every few minutes to turn the potatoes over until they're done, 20 minutes or a little more, depending on the size and heft of the pot and potatoes. They'll be ready when a paring knife slides through easily. It's unlikely, by the way, that they'll be charred evenly all over, but that won't matter. Serve them whole.

For the radicchio

Core the heads of the radicchio, pull off the coarse outer leaves, rinse, and shake dry. Cut each head into halves or quarters, depending on their size, and set them center side up in a pan that can go under the broiler. Drizzle lightly with olive oil and lemon juice, then sprinkle a tiny bit of salt and grind a good amount of pepper over it. Begin broiling—you can broil this with the steak, if you have room—and when the radicchio begins to char on top, push it around with a long fork or wooden spoon in order to expose more of the leaves to the direct heat. When the radicchio is thoroughly wilted and blackened on top, it's ready. Keep warm until ready to serve.

2 fist-size heads of radicchio
3 tablespoons olive oil
Juice of 1 lemon
Salt and freshly ground pepper

For the chutney

Spoon Major Grey's from the bottle into a bowl, or else put a dollop on everyone's plate.

Add-a-Course Notes

First course: Caesar Salad, page 185.

Dessert: Apple Tart, page 189.

he word "bouillabaisse" translates roughly to mean boil *(bouille)*, then lower *(baisse)*. Classic bouillabaisse is boiled at the highest heat possible to draw the flavor of the fish into the broth, then the heat is lowered. With this version, the heating requirements aren't nearly so dramatic.

Making a classic bouillabaisse is like undertaking a sacred ritual, and requires—for starters—boiling fish, or at least fish heads, all day long in order to make the stock. (The version below requires no such thing.) Even among denizens of the Mediterranean,

Menu

s e r v e s   s i x

Bouillabaisse for Beginners

Mixed Green Salad with Scallions, Walnuts, Gorgonzola, and Pears, in a Mustard-Balsamic Vinaigrette

birthplace of bouillabaisse, there is great disagreement as to how it should be made: with which kinds of fish? with potatoes or not? But since the local fish caught daily along the Mediterranean aren't ever available to us, that shouldn't be a quibble. Should you be serving dinner to a real French cook, I'd advise against serving anything remotely French; otherwise this simple fish stew is always a success.

The basic drill is this: Into a soup or pasta bowl you put a slice of toasted baguette spread with rouille, a garlicky mayonnaise made orange-red with the addition of pimentos; the fish stew gets ladled over the toast so that the color and flavor of the rouille also infuse the stew.

This version calls for chicken stock (canned!) instead of fish stock, in the theory that the fish itself makes the stew fishy enough. It's also a heartier version than some, with the addition of a lot of finely chopped vegetables, which also intensify the broth.

If the thought of making a bouillabaisse sounds daunting, just think of it as fish stew, which is what it was until it got fancy. Don't worry too much about getting the fish measurements exactly right; if you want, you can mix and match; try not to omit the shrimp, though, and especially the clams—you want to see clamshells in the soup. This recipe will serve about six. Thin it out with a little more stock and a little more of each fish, and it will serve eight. It's also easily doubled, even if you have to make it in two pots.

For the bouillabaisse

1 stalk celery

1 big carrot, peeled

1 big Spanish onion, peeled

4 big cloves garlic, peeled

1 fennel bulb, optional

Olive oil

One 35-ounce can whole peeled tomatoes, with their juice

1 cup dry white wine

Three 10 ½-ounce cans chicken broth (and 1 backup, in case you need it)

Generous pinch saffron or cayenne pepper

18 shrimp, give or take, peeled and deveined

18 littleneck clams, give or take, in their shells

½ pound bay scallops

1 pound firm-fleshed fish (such as halibut, snapper, or cod), cut up into big bite-size pieces

Handful of fresh basil

Freshly ground pepper

This may look like a lot of ingredients, but don't let that throw you; most of them are vegetables.

In a food processor, chop the celery, carrot, onion, and fennel into bits each about the size of a raisin. You want them still to have some bite, crunch, and distinction—so don't pulverize them into a paste. Mince the garlic.

Coat the bottom of a big pot generously with the olive oil, throw in the chopped vegetables and sauté over medium heat until they begin to soften around the edges, about 5 minutes. Chop the tomatoes coarsely and add them with their juice, the wine, 3 cans broth, and saffron or cayenne pepper to the pot. Bring the liquid to a boil (bouille) for a few minutes—about 3—then reduce it to a low-bubble simmer (baisse). It needs to simmer for about 45 minutes.

Meanwhile you might want to make the rouille (see below). You could also slice and toast the baguette at this point, allowing at least one slice of bread per person, since the bread doesn't have to be hot when you serve it.

After 45 minutes or so, toss in all the seafood and fish, raising the heat to high against this onslaught. There should still be enough liquid to suggest a soup or stew thick enough that each ladleful will yield some fish and vegetables; if there isn't, add another can of broth. When the mixture reaches a boil again, reduce the heat back to where it was and cover. When the clams open, which should take 10 minutes or so (discard any that don't open), snip in the fresh basil, grind in some fresh pepper to taste, stir again, and serve.

Add-a-Course Notes

First course: Seasonal Remoulade, page 182.

Dessert: Demitasse Chocolate, page 192.

For the rouille

Measure the bread crumbs first (so they won't stick to the olive oil) into the bowl of the food processor, then add the oil, pimentos, garlic, basil, and cayenne, along with a dash of salt and a few grindings of black pepper. Process thoroughly until you've got a mayonnaiselike consistency.

Spread the rouille on the toast, place the toast in the bottom of the soup or pasta bowls, place equal portions of the fish around the toast, ladle the soup over the bread, and pretend you're in the Mediterranean.

¼ cup bread crumbs
⅓ cup olive oil
One 2-ounce jar pimentos, drained
4 cloves garlic
5 or 6 basil leaves
¼ teaspoon cayenne pepper
Salt and freshly ground pepper
6 slices toasted baguette

For the salad

Clean the lettuce, slice the scallions—white and green parts both. When you're ready to serve the salad, toss the greens with the vinaigrette (below). Don't slice the pears until the very last minute, or they'll discolor. When you're ready, core and slice them lengthwise into fairly narrow strips. Toss the salad. Put the pears on next, then the crumbled cheese, then the walnuts. *Don't* toss again. As you're serving the salad, the vinaigrette will work its way just enough into the pears, cheese, and nuts. Serve the salad as a separate course.

2 heads green leaf lettuce
1 bunch scallions
3 pears
Modest pie-slice of Gorgonzola, crumbled
Handful of shelled, coarsely chopped walnuts

For the vinaigrette

Whisk all the ingredients together until blended.

¼ cup olive oil
2 tablespoons balsamic vinegar
1 teaspoon dry mustard
Sprinkling of salt
1 teaspoon or more freshly ground pepper

he idea for chicken roasted in this unusual way came from a cookbook by Caroline Blackwood and Anna Haycraft called *Darling, You Shouldn't Have Gone to So Much Trouble,* which was published in England but never in America. Among other cut-corner ideas, it includes a splendid recipe called The Earl of Gowrie's Fowl, which, because it calls for just two main ingredients, one being the fowl itself, caught my eye at once. If you work fast, the prep time for this roast chicken can be reduced to about ninety seconds.

That the first of these two ingredients was pheasant didn't deter me in the least—a fowl is essentially a fowl, and my shortcut-seeking mind had already jumped ahead to substituting chicken, although you could certainly use pheasant if you had one around. It was the second ingredient—garlic

Menu

serves six

Roast Chicken with a
Surprise Ingredient

Skillet Potato Tart

String Beans with
Ground Fennel

Boursin—that captured my imagination. Chicken stuffed with Boursin. The cheese melts, the book said, and, scooped from the cavity when the chicken is done and whisked with the pan juices, it makes a creamy and delicious sauce. The book's right.

Any kind of Boursin or Boursin-type cheese will do (doesn't have to be garlic), and once it melts into the sauce, no one will guess what it is—plus the chicken will be infused with a marvelous herbal essence. To serve four, you'll need a three- or four-pound chicken and one cake of cheese. To serve six, you'll need a five- or six-pound chicken; here, the sauce will taste better if you use two cakes of Boursin so that the cavity is filled with it. This will make a lot of sauce, more than you'll need, and I've never figured out what to do with the leftover sauce, which seems pretty fattening by the next day. Nevertheless, this dish is a great (and easy!) once-in-a-while extravagance.

As for the potato tart, it's deceptively simple to make, glorious to present, and delicious. I use a big cast-iron skillet, which comes right to the table still bubbling. The thin potato slices (which take no time to prepare with a mandoline) are arranged to look like a pretty apple tart, in tightly overlapping concentric circles, and you cut the tart like a pie when it's ready. If you're going to be cooking the chicken and potato tart in the same oven, arrange the racks to accommodate both before you preheat it, then put the tart in an hour before the chicken is due to be ready. The string beans are self-explanatory, except that for some reason they taste good with ground fennel from a jar.

For the chicken

1 roasting chicken,
approximately 5 to 6 pounds
1 to 2 packages Boursin
cheese, any kind
Tiny bit of dry white wine or
chicken broth
1 smallish Spanish onion
Juice of half a lemon
Salt and freshly ground
black pepper

Preheat the oven to 450°F. Rinse the chicken and pat it as dry as you can with paper towels (cloth dishtowels might pick up any bacteria lurking around). Stuff the cavity, the fuller the better, with the Boursin (unwrapped from the tin foil), pull up that little flap of skin just below the cavity, and tie the legs together with twine. Put the chicken into a roasting pan, preferably one not much bigger than the chicken itself.

Pour enough wine or broth into the roasting pan just to cover the bottom. Chop the onion medium fine, and put it in the roasting pan around the chicken. Drizzle the lemon juice over the top of the chicken, then add a minimalist sprinkling of salt and a generous amount of pepper.

Put the chicken into the oven, and lower the heat to 350°F right now, before you forget. Roast the chicken at 350°F for 20 minutes per pound. The way to tell it's finished is to prick the skin where the leg meets the rest of the chicken. When the juices that seep out are clear, the chicken is cooked. The way to gain confidence in this technique is to try it out about an hour ahead of when the chicken should be ready. You'll see that the juices are pink; by the time they run clear, you'll be able to see the difference.

Let the chicken sit for 10 minutes before carving it. Meanwhile, cut or untie the string, spoon out the Boursin, whisk it together with the pan juices and onion, put it into a gravy boat or whatever you're going to serve it in, and keep it warm until you're ready to serve it.

For the potato tart

Don't bother to peel the potatoes, but slice them very thin, like potato chips, preferably with a mandoline. Throw away the small ends; the potato slices should be relatively uniform in size. Put the slices into a bowl of ice water to leach excess starch from the potatoes for at least 10 minutes.

Peel the garlic, cut the cloves in half, and rub the cut sides over a large cast-iron skillet, a pie pan, or any large round or oval thing you can put into the oven. Now rub 2 tablespoons of the butter over the bottom of the skillet and up the sides, to prevent the tart-to-be from sticking.

Dump the ice water from the bowl with the potato slices in it, and rinse the slices in cold water for a while to wash the starch off. Now—this is the tedious part—dry the slices. You'll be surprised at how hard this is to do, as drops of water will keep turning up on them in an annoying way. I usually blot them between two clean bath towels.

Now—this is the fun part—arrange the slices tightly and evenly in overlapping concentric circles, from the outer edges of the pan into the center, to make the tart look pretty; allow only a fraction of an inch of each slice to show—you want to use up all the slices. When the slices are all in place, blot once more from the top with a towel, pressing down hard. Whisk together the egg and cream, and pour over the tart, distributing it as evenly as you can (the egg-cream mixture probably won't cover the whole tart, but don't worry about that). Dot with tiny bits of the remaining tablespoon of butter here and there, and sprinkle lightly with salt, and grind on lots of pepper, and I mean lots. (Don't put the salt and pepper into the egg mixture—you want them to stay where you sprinkle or grind them.)

Bake at 350°F for 1 hour, or until the edges of the potato slices are beginning to brown. Then put the tart under the broiler until it's browned and bubbly all over. Bring to the table as is to present it, then cut into wedges and serve.

6 medium potatoes
3 cloves garlic
3 tablespoons unsalted butter
1 egg
2 to 3 tablespoons
  heavy cream
Salt and freshly ground pepper

For the string beans

6 handfuls string beans
Salt
Butter
Sprinkling of ground fennel
Freshly ground pepper

Put the string beans, ends cut off, into a small amount of boiling water, just enough to steam them, to which you've added a pinch of salt. I like to use a bigger pan than seems necessary, so as to spread the beans out as much as possible. Taste them frequently until you find that the raw taste has gone away, and they're just short of being fully cooked. Drain the water out quickly, spread on a pat of butter, sprinkle on a pinch of ground fennel, a tiny bit of salt, and as many grindings of pepper as you like. Cover tightly; the heat remaining in the string beans will finish cooking them, and they'll stay warm for a good 10 or 15 minutes besides.

To cook them in the microwave, place the string beans (ends cut off) neatly on a microwave-safe platter, sprinkle on 5 or 6 drops of water, and cover tightly with plastic wrap. Cooking time will vary, depending on the quantity of string beans and the microwave itself. In mine, this would take 5 or 6 minutes. When they're cooked (they cook beautifully in the microwave, and stay bright green), toss in the butter, ground fennel, salt, and pepper. Re-cover with plastic wrap until you're ready to serve. If they're cool, reheat in the microwave before serving.

Add-a-Course Notes

First course: Seafood Salad, page 171.

Dessert: Suzanne's Blueberry (Cake Mix) Cobbler, page 188.

*I*t's been said that you can gauge the quality of a restaurant by the coffee it serves. To put a twist on this, I think that if a home cook can pull off a recipe familiar to restaurant-goers, it suggests that he or she has an easy confidence that seems almost professional. Linguine with clam sauce is a case in point, great Italian bistro fare that can be made perfectly well at home. If yours compares favorably with that served at popular local hangouts, then your dining room could also become a lively local hangout, if that's what you're after.

There are probably as many recipes for linguine with clam sauce as there are cooks who make it, but mine works as well as any—it's good. One shortcut here is not chopping up the garlic but sautéing the peeled cloves whole: This method (which also works in most other recipes calling for garlic sautéed in oil) makes it less likely that you'll burn the garlic, which tastes awful, plus it saves you the trouble of mincing garlic in the first place. The garlic taste comes through fine.

Menu

serves four

Linguine with Clam Sauce

Green Salad with a Honeyed Vinaigrette and Warmed Goat Cheese

Bread, if you want

Because it's a culinary faux pas to offer Parmesan with most seafood pastas, it works well to serve a salad with cheese separately, as a course following the linguine. You could also marinate the sliced goat cheese in olive oil and roll it in bread crumbs before broiling, but this way is lighter. The dressing, sweetened slightly with honey, is a good contrast to the clam sauce, which even without adding one grain of salt tastes like the sea. You can serve the bread with either course.

For the clam sauce

3 dozen cherrystone clams
1 cup dry white wine
4 cloves garlic, peeled
but not chopped
Olive oil
½ teaspoon red
pepper flakes
Freshly ground black pepper
4 tablespoons fresh oregano
leaves (or an equivalent mix
of oregano leaves, chopped
chives, and
parsley, or fresh basil, if
that's all that's around)
1 pound linguine

Rinse off the clams to remove any sand clinging to them, put into a big stockpot with a lid, pour in the wine, turn the heat to high, and cover. When the liquid begins to boil, turn the heat down to medium. Check the clams every few minutes and, when the ones on top are partway open, after 10 minutes, give or take, turn off the heat and remove the cover to let them cool. The less open they are the better—even if you have to wrestle with them a bit to remove the clams from the shell; they shouldn't overcook.

Meanwhile, take a big fry pan (I use one big enough to accommodate the pasta itself, and serve the dish on a trivet right from the pan: This meal is *informal*), cover the bottom of it generously with olive oil, and sauté the garlic cloves till they're browned on all sides, then discard the garlic and turn off the burner.

When the clams have cooled, remove them from their shells, taking care not to throw any of the broth away; the broth is the essence of the sauce. It's best just to scoop the clams from their shells with a paring knife or clam knife right over the stockpot itself, so that the broth falls right back in. Any clams that absolutely refuse to open should be thrown away.

Pour the broth into the pan with the olive oil, add the red pepper flakes, grind in some pepper, and bring the mixture to a boil. Boil it for a while as the broth reduces and intensifies. How long will vary, because sometimes you get more liquid than others, but a 7- to 10-minute boil will usually do it. What you want is to see the grayish broth with swirls of golden oil throughout, and to have enough liquid in which to toss the pasta without having pools of it on the bottom of the bowls or plates. Taste it to see whether there's enough red pepper flavor and, if there isn't, sprinkle in a bit more, remembering that the pepper flavor gets stronger the more the sauce boils.

Once the sauce is reduced—and when you've put the linguine in to cook—turn the heat to low, chop the clams in halves or thirds, and add them to the sauce to just heat them through. Snip the herb or herbs in coarsely, toss in the cooked pasta, and serve.

For the salad

4 big handfuls mixed greens, cleaned
Two 3-ounce logs goat cheese

For the vinaigrette

2 tablespoons olive oil
2 tablespoons vegetable oil
1 tablespoon white wine
*   vinegar*
2 tablespoons honey
Freshly ground pepper

Whisk the ingredients together and taste. You may want a little more vinegar or honey. (Goat cheese is salted, so don't salt the vinaigrette.)

Cut each log of cheese in half, flatten slightly to make a patty, and place them on a cookie sheet that's been covered with tin foil. Put this under the broiler and, watching carefully, remove it as the cheese begins to deflate a little but before it starts to melt and lose its shape. You just want it *warmed*, not turned into a puddle. Toss the greens in the vinaigrette, divide among four plates, place the cheese on top of the greens in the middle of the plate, and serve while the cheese is still warm.

Add-a-Course Notes

First course: Sizzled, Flavored Meat on Shredded Lettuce, page 181.

Dessert: Pear Crisp, page 195.

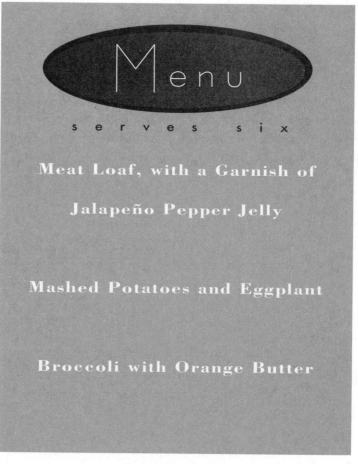

I remember as a child being given meat loaf made by various friends' mothers, and wanting to, well, flee; I liked only my mother's meat loaf. For that matter, my friends probably liked only *their* mothers' meat loaves, too, and to this day most cooks probably still cook only their mothers' meat loaf, which limits the pass-around possibilities for other good recipes. Still, I stand by my mother's recipe (I've changed it only slightly, to make it more fattening), which uses Wheaties instead of the usual bread crumbs, thus giving it a less crumbly texture than most versions. Cornflakes would work, too. So would other kinds of barbecue sauces, but Open Pit Original is the one that really tastes like home to me. As for the pepper jelly (available at most gourmet shops and some supermarkets), a spoonful of it is an excellent accompaniment—to anyone's meat loaf. It's also good spread on bread the next day for meat-loaf sandwiches.

I've found that a wooden salad bowl is a great place in which to mix the meat loaf, putting the meat in first, making a hole in the middle, adding the rest of the ingre-

Menu

serves six

Meat Loaf, with a Garnish of Jalapeño Pepper Jelly

Mashed Potatoes and Eggplant

Broccoli with Orange Butter

dients before mixing with your hands, and washing the bowl well (obviously) in soap and very hot water afterward. I'm sure there are people who would say this is dangerous because of bacteria or whatever; the way I see it is that there's also a risk that a plane might fall on your head while you're cooking. Besides, the latest research shows well-washed wood to be perfectly safe for chopping. And butchers have been using wooden shambles (those thick butcher-block tables; that's where the phrase that something "is a shambles" comes from) for centuries. So I feel safe using a salad bowl for mixing, but it might just be that I like to live dangerously.

The potato-eggplant dish was inspired by a similar dish served at the Union Square Cafe in New York City. This recipe is what I ended up with when I tried to re-create it at home; it's not exactly the same, but a good facsimile. The orange-sweetened butter for the broccoli is a good counterpoint to the spicier potatoes and eggplant, and the pepper jelly.

For the meat loaf

(Step one: Take off any rings you happen to be wearing. The only way to mix this is with your hands, and meat loaf has a way of working itself into rings and staying there for days.)

Preheat the oven to 350°F. Add all the ingredients except the bacon to the meat; mush it all together; shape into a loaf in a baking pan with sides, to catch the grease that drains out. Arrange the slices of bacon on top. Cut into it to check for doneness after 45 minutes, but it might take up to an hour to just cook all the way through. Discard the bacon and grease when it's done, and let the loaf cool for 5 or 10 minutes to "set" before slicing.

2 pounds, give or take, ground round
1 big Spanish onion, chopped pretty fine
1 egg
1 1/4 cups Wheaties
Several dashes Worcestershire sauce
Salt and freshly ground pepper
1/4 to 3/4 cup Open Pit Original barbecue sauce (depending on whether the quantity of meat is under or over)
1 cup grated cheddar cheese
3 or 4 strips bacon

For the eggplant-potatoes

2 good-size eggplants
6 potatoes
Big chunk of fresh ginger
4 tablespoons olive oil
3 cloves garlic, peeled
but left whole
4 tablespoons butter
½ cup heavy cream
Hot chili sesame oil
Salt and freshly ground pepper
Bottled sliced ginger for garnish
(optional)

Cut the eggplants in half lengthwise, put them skin side down on a cookie sheet in a 350°F oven, and cook for 20 to 30 minutes, until they're visibly deflated.

Quarter the unpeeled potatoes, cover with water, and throw in 4 or 5 slices of ginger, each as thick as a quarter. No need to peel the ginger, which will give a gingery aura to the potatoes. Cook at a gentle boil for 20 minutes, or until a paring knife can slide through easily.

In the pan in which you plan to make the dish, heat the olive oil and sauté the garlic cloves and 3 or 4 slices of ginger (unpeeled again is fine) until they're lightly browned, then discard.

Once the potatoes are cooked, rinse them in cold water, and put them through a potato ricer or a food mill, or mash them with a hand masher, discarding the peel. (Don't use a food processor, however tempting, which will turn them into potato glue.) As for the now-cooked eggplant, scoop out the pulp, throw away the skin, and mash the pulp either in a food processor or with a potato masher. You could use a fork, but it would take a long time to get the lumps out.

Now stir the mashed potatoes and eggplant together into the garlic-ginger oil, add the butter, cream, a few dashes of hot chili sesame oil, salt, and pepper; you can fluff them up by beating vigorously with a wooden spoon or a potato masher. To garnish with the bottled ginger, roll up a slice of it atop each portion—but you don't have to.

For the broccoli

Remove coarse outer leaves on the broccoli stalks, cut off the bottoms, and halve the stalks lengthwise or, if they're really big, cut them into thirds.

To cook them the conventional way, in a big frying pan bring enough water, to which you've added a pinch of salt, to a boil. When the water begins to boil, lay the stalks as flat as you can on the bottom, crisscrossing so that the florets aren't all piled up. Cover. Check after 4 minutes by piercing with a paring knife. When it pierces the stalk without resistance but still feels al dente, drain out the water and leave covered until ready to serve, at which time move the broccoli to a platter or put it on the plates.

To microwave, crisscross the stalks on a platter, with the floret ends arranged on the *outside* of the platter. Sprinkle 4 or 5 drops of water over the broccoli, then cover tightly with plastic wrap. Microwave times vary, but check it after 3 or 4 minutes to see how it's doing. Again, cook until it's al dente. Leave tightly covered in plastic wrap until you're ready to serve it.

Meanwhile, bring the orange juice to a boil, and boil until it's reduced to about 1/4 cup; it will be slightly glazy by then and, if you've used fresh juice, some of the residue will have stuck to the sides of the pan. This is okay. Swirl the remaining juice around and push the residue down into the juice as best you can with a wooden spoon or plastic spatula. Sprinkle with salt and pepper to taste. Whisk in the butter, and pour the juice evenly over the drained broccoli.

6 stalks broccoli, or however many you think
Salt (optional)
1 cup orange juice, preferably freshly squeezed (but it doesn't have to be)
2 tablespoons butter
Freshly ground pepper

Add-a-Course Notes

First course: Smoked Salmon with Dilled Honey-Mustard Sauce, page 177.

Dessert: Cherry Clafouti, page 196.

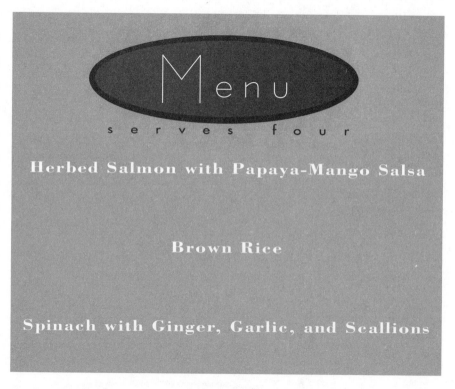

xcept for finely chopping the ingredients for the salsa, which is tedious, this is a relatively painless dinner to make, pretty to look at, clean-tasting, and with a surprising mix of tastes and textures. If you make it in the winter, it somehow reminds you that spring is on the way; served in summer, it's very cooling.

Fruit salsas are relatively new to most of us, but are finding their way more and more onto the menus of the finer California-type restaurants, so it's just as well to know how to make one at home. In the summertime, fresh peaches or apricots are also wonderful in fruit salsas.

Menu

serves four

Herbed Salmon with Papaya-Mango Salsa

Brown Rice

Spinach with Ginger, Garlic, and Scallions

I've specified brown rice for this menu rather than white, because brown rice has a bite and weightiness to it that seem to anchor the rest of the meal, which is very light; fruit and spinach are, after all, largely comprised of water. What is more, if you read about rice, you'll learn that every time it's hybridized, supposedly to make it better for one reason or another, it becomes less nutritious; brown rice is at least refined less than white. Brown basmati rice would also work here. As for the spinach, adding ginger to the mix seems to tie it in with the rest of the menu.

For the salsa

Chop everything except the cilantro and stir together. Refrigerate for a little while so the flavors will blend before adding the cilantro and spooning over the cooked fish at the very last minute.

If you make extra, it will keep for 2 or 3 days; again, add the cilantro at the last minute.

4 tablespoons finely diced mango
4 tablespoons finely diced papaya
4 tablespoons finely diced cucumber
4 tablespoons finely diced red onion
1 fresh jalapeño pepper, diced, or 2 tablespoons from a jar
1 tablespoon white vinegar
2 tablespoons vegetable oil
Salt and freshly ground pepper
2 tablespoons chopped cilantro, added at the last minute

For the salmon

Get the broiler going. Drizzle the lemon or lime juice over the salmon and spread it around with your fingers. Sprinkle or rub the cumin and the ginger over it as well, and grind some pepper over it, too. Broil, skin side down, in a broiler-worthy tray until the salmon is crispy-looking on top and still pink in the middle. Cut into it after about 5 minutes to see how it's doing; salmon doesn't take very long to cook. Once it's ready, carefully cut the fillet into quarters, sliding each off the skin (this isn't hard, much easier, in fact, than dicing all that fruit), arrange on a platter with lime wedges. (If you have any cilantro left over, you might as well put sprigs of it on the platter, too, as a garnish, since fresh cilantro doesn't keep well at all.

Drizzle of lemon or lime juice
1½ pounds salmon fillet, with the skin left on
1 teaspoon ground cumin
2 teaspoons ground ginger
Freshly ground pepper
Lime wedges, for garnish

For the rice

Follow the directions on the box.

For the spinach

Vegetable oil
3 cloves garlic, peeled
but not minced
3 quarter-size pieces fresh
ginger, unpeeled (but with
ginger exposed on
both sides)
10 ounces fresh spinach,
washed and dried
as best you can
2 scallions, diced fairly fine
(slicing them on the bias
looks particularly elegant)
Salt and freshly ground
pepper

Unless you're as fond of it as Popeye is, approximately 10 ounces of fresh (or one 10-ounce box of frozen) spinach should serve four.

Swish a minimal amount of vegetable oil around to cover the bottom and coat the sides of a wok or fry pan and sauté the garlic and ginger in the oil until browned, then remove and throw them away. You'll have the garlic-ginger taste, but with no chance of burning the garlic and without having to peel and mince the ginger. While the salmon is broiling, toss the spinach and scallions in the oil until the spinach is wilted and looks more or less cooked. Sprinkle with salt, grind some pepper on, toss again, and serve.

Add-a-Course Notes

First course: Pizza, page 179.

Dessert: Suzanne's Honeyed Cheese, page 188.

ost of us probably eat boneless breasts of chicken, served one way or another, at least once a week, and can never find enough ways to vary the theme. They're like classic black dresses—you can accessorize them any which way. One trick is to examine every recipe you run across from a boneless breast of chicken point of view; very often, particularly with fish or veal or pork recipes, they'll work just as well with chicken. I was first served some version of this mushroom sauce piled on veal scaloppine, for example, in a pretty dreadful restaurant, but liked the idea and made the leap to chicken scaloppine.

By mixing fresh (and cheaper) mushrooms with a few of the stronger dried (more intense and expensive) ones, you infuse the dried mushroom taste into them all, giving an earthiness to the simple chicken. Adding the toast underneath—a thick piece of toasted Tuscan or peasant bread—was my idea, to creatively layer the dish and give it more texture and some crunch. Plus, bread dipped in essence

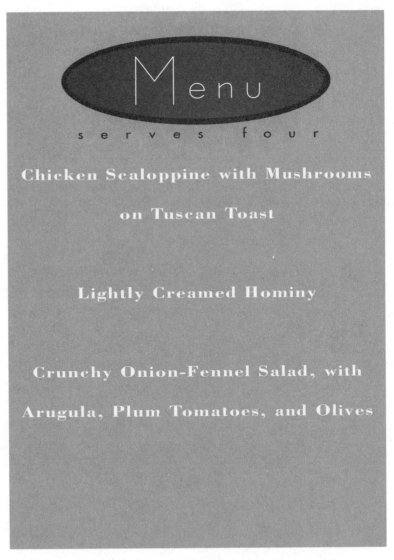

Menu

serves four

Chicken Scaloppine with Mushrooms

on Tuscan Toast

Lightly Creamed Hominy

Crunchy Onion-Fennel Salad, with

Arugula, Plum Tomatoes, and Olives

of mushrooms is as good as bread dipped in just about anything. The hominy, made right from the can, is sweeter and nutty, in good contrast to the moodiness of the mushrooms.

The salad is a cheerful, colorful, crunchy affair, which really deserves to be served before or after the entree as a separate course, or definitely on a separate salad plate. It calls for vegetable oil because sometimes it's nice not to have *every* salad taste of olive oil; red wine vinegar has a less distinctive taste than, say, balsamic—and here you want the vinaigrette to "dress" the salad down, and sweeten it, not dress it up the way you might with a simple green salad. You can, however, use whatever oil and vinegar you happen to have around.

For the chicken and mushroom sauce

2 shallots
3 tablespoons butter
2 tablespoons vegetable oil
4 chicken scaloppine,
or 2 boned,
skinned chicken breasts
1 ounce dried mushrooms,
any kind
1 average-size supermarket
box fresh mushrooms,
about 4 per person
Few drops of balsamic
vinegar
1 tablespoon heavy cream
Salt and freshly
ground pepper
1 round loaf peasant bread
(with crispy crust)

For the chicken itself, chop the shallots fine, and sauté them in a fry pan (a cast-iron skillet is good for this, but any fry pan will do) in 1 tablespoon of the butter and the 2 tablespoons of vegetable oil. When the shallots are golden, add the chicken scaloppine or chicken breasts and sauté on both sides on medium-high heat until they're just cooked through. Slice into thin strips and set aside.

Add enough water to cover and just a little bit more to the dried mushrooms—just a little; you don't want them to look like swimmers floating in a pool. Blot the fresh mushrooms clean with a damp paper towel, cut off the bottoms of the stems (*why* do we have to cut off the bottoms? Sometimes, I admit, I skip that step, so far with no ill results), and slice. Begin to sauté them in a hot fry pan in the remaining 2 tablespoons of butter. Once they turn mahogany colored and begin to release their juices, dump in the juice from the dried mushrooms, pressing them hard in order to release all the juice. (It doesn't hurt to put the juice through a strainer first, in case there are any lingering bits of earth.) Now mince the dried mushrooms, add them to the pan, stir, and keep on cooking at medium to high until all the juice is absorbed. Stir in a few drops of balsamic vinegar (this gives the mushrooms almost a glazed look) and the heavy cream, to sweeten and smooth out the flavor, add salt and pepper to taste, and that's pretty much it.

For the toast, cut the bread into slices more or less the size of the scaloppine. As for thickness, not too thick: You want the chicken to look as if it's resting on a cushion, not a full-size mattress and box spring. Toast it.

Toast goes on the bottom, chicken in the middle, mushrooms on top.

For the hominy

Open the cans, drain the hominy, put it into a food processor, and pulse until it's the texture of coarse-ground meal; or you could mash it with a potato masher. Heat it up with the butter and cream to bind and flavor it, add a little salt and a few grindings of pepper, sprinkle the chives on top, and serve with the chicken, etc.

Two 16-ounce cans hominy
1 to 2 tablespoons butter
1 to 2 tablespoons heavy cream
Salt and freshly ground pepper
Fresh chives (or finely chopped green parts of scallions) to sprinkle on top

For the dressing

Make the dressing first, so that the fennel and onion can marinate in it a while; the dressing will sweeten the onion and take the raw edge off the fennel. Whisk all the ingredients together, taste, and add more oil, vinegar, or mustard to suit your taste.

½ cup vegetable oil
3 tablespoons red wine vinegar
1 teaspoon dry mustard
Salt and freshly ground pepper

For the salad

1 fennel bulb
1 medium onion
4 to 6 plum tomatoes
1 big bunch arugula, washed free of any gritty dirt
Generous handful or so of black olives (I use the wrinkly Moroccan ones)

Cut off the very bottom of the fennel, and slice the bulb very thin; a mandoline or food slicer will enable you to do this in seconds. Same with the onion—slice it very thin, preferably with a mandoline. Toss the mixture together with the dressing; it can marinate like this for up to a couple of hours, either in the fridge or at room temperature; it doesn't really matter.

Chop the tomatoes at the last minute and add them, along with the arugula, to the salad. Put the olives on top, and that's about it.

Add-a-Course Notes

First course: Christopher's Smoked Fish Salad, page 173.

Dessert: Sweetened Ricotta and Mixed Fruit, page 191.

Pork tenderloin is a boon to lazy cooks. It's inexpensive, relatively low-fat—all the things those cheerful pork ads promise. You can cook it in various ways, wrapped around dried fruits, for instance, or baked in milk (to tenderize and sweeten it). It's simplest broiled, and even more delicious cooked on an outdoor grill. All the worries about eating undercooked pork seem to me exaggerated: Just cook it all the way through, that's all, and cut into the middle of it to be sure it's done. (We don't avoid chicken because *it* has to be cooked all the way through, do we?) Like chicken, too, pork is a good vehicle for carrying sauces.

I'm happy with many of the meats at the supermarket, but I prefer to buy pork from the butcher; in my experience it just tastes better. Besides, the butcher will cut the loin—tell him you want it boneless—to accommodate the number of people you're serving and also cut the loin into single-serving medallions, if that's what you want. (For variety, you can then—or the butcher will—pound the medallions flat and cook them like scaloppine.)

Grilling pork the way it's called for here is like grilling (or broiling) anything else. It's pretty

Menu

s e r v e s   s i x

Grilled Pork Loin with Onion-Sage Sauce Served on a Bed of Watercress

Pineapple Chutney

Curried Basmati Rice

String Beans with Pine Nuts

served on watercress, and the onion sauce, as you'll see, is hardly backbreaking, and can also be served on chicken, turkey, or fish. The pineapple chutney is my mother's recipe; we had it with ham every Easter when I was growing up, and other times, when we could persuade her to make it. When I serve it now, people think it's very gourmet. Pine nuts on string beans are simply a variation of the old string beans and slivered almonds routine.

For the pork loin

4 pounds pork loin, approximately
Olive oil
1 bunch watercress

Brush the pork with the olive oil, then put it on the grill or under the broiler, fat side exposed to the heat first. If you're using a broiler, don't put it *directly* under, but one rack below that. When the fat side is browned, turn it over, brushing both sides with oil again as you do it. On the grill; the loin should be cooked through in about half an hour (check it from time to time after 15 minutes); the broiler will take a little longer. When it comes time to serve it, slice it and spread the slices over watercress and ladle the sauce over that.

For the onion sauce

One 10-ounce package frozen baby onions in cream sauce
Pinch of ground sage
Pinch of salt
Freshly ground pepper
2 tablespoons heavy cream

Cook the onions in the microwave or on the stove, according to the directions on the package. Put in a blender or food processor and blend or pulse until smooth. Add the rest of the ingredients. Bingo!

For the pineapple chutney

Preheat the oven to 350°F. Mix all the ingredients together, adding the beaten eggs last. Pour into a greased casserole or some kind of ovenproof thing and bake for about 50 minutes, until the dish sets.

One 20-ounce can crushed pineapple with the juice
¼ cup sugar
2 tablespoons cornstarch
¼ cup water
1 teaspoon vanilla extract
2 eggs, beaten with a fork or an egg beater until frothy

For the basmati rice

Cook the rice according to the package directions. Fluff it up when cooked and stir in the other ingredients, adding more curry if you like, to taste. The vegetable oil will stretch the effects of the butter.

2 cups basmati rice
2 tablespoons vegetable oil
1 tablespoon butter
1 teaspoon curry powder

For the string beans

Follow instructions for cooking string beans (page 76). Toast the pine nuts (page 63). When the beans are ready, drizzle very lightly with olive oil, sprinkle with salt, grind on some pepper, and sprinkle pine nuts on top.

6 handfuls string beans
3 tablespoons pine nuts
Olive oil
Salt and freshly ground pepper

Add-a-Course Notes

First course: Seafood Salad, page 171.

Dessert: Peter's Chocolate Cake, page 194.

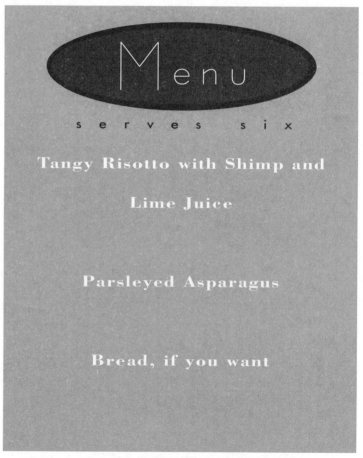

I once met a man who worked in advertising and who said, when asked, that he thought the classic commercials for Minute Rice—"Perfect rice every time"—were the most brilliant ads ever written. Why? Because for the first time in the entire history of food they raised the possibility of *im*perfect rice, giving rise to the myth, one that still plagues insecure cooks, that rice is hard to make. It's not. With all the new basmati/jasmati white, brown, and mixed cultivars available, it's essential to overcome Fear of Rice if you want to be perceived as a good cook. Not counting the minute rices, there are hundreds of kinds of rice worldwide, and all are cooked the same way: Simply.

The rice that intimidates people the most, I think, is arborio rice, the kind used to make risotto—itself a concept that scares all too many cooks as well. It needn't, however, because getting the hang of cooking risotto is no harder than learning to cook pasta al dente. Easier, actually, because risotto cooks slowly and allows more room for leeway: There's no *now!* moment of rushing around ("Oh, God, where's the colander?") the way there is with pasta, which is ready one minute, overcooked the next. With risotto, once it's ready, you still have a few minutes to get your act together. It's that relaxed.

Menu

s e r v e s   s i x

Tangy Risotto with Shimp and Lime Juice

Parsleyed Asparagus

Bread, if you want

Arborio rice is short and plump, and gets even plumper, not to mention creamy (because of the starch it releases) as you slowly add liquid for it to absorb—like filling a balloon, in a way—and cook it slowly, over low heat. You start by adding a cup or more of wine, then fill the rest of the rice up with broth, all very slowly; arborio rice soaks up a surprising amount of liquid. Why does the liquid have to be added slowly? I don't know; it just does. Does it have to be stirred continually, as the recipes say? Not continually, but at least every few minutes. You can putter around doing other things, stir for a minute, putter, stir, putter, stir, and so on. How long does the actual intense stirring really take? Usually between twenty and thirty minutes, depending on how many people you're stirring for and how much other stuff—meat, fish, vegetables—is going into the dish. Is there a way to jump-start the process? Yes. (Some cooks do so in the microwave, but this method doesn't save as much time as you'd think, and anyway, you have to keep putting it in and taking it out of the microwave to stir it, which also takes a lot of time. What is more, you lose the important aroma of the risotto infusing the kitchen. I'd rather use the microwave for the asparagus.)

The Italians nearly always serve risotto as a first course, but we upstart New Worlders have found that there's no reason at all not to serve it as an entree, the gourmet update of the old-fashioned one-dish casserole. Just add bread and a salad or vegetable, and you have a perfect family meal.

Like pasta, risotto can be flavored probably hundreds of ways, and even canned or frozen ingredients can rise to the occasion. While in many cookbooks people are forever dropping by unexpectedly for dinner, I have found that in real life (my life, anyway) few people are actually that rude. Such impromptu affairs do generate spontaneously sometimes, however, and last winter I found myself with no plans one minute, and four people coming for dinner in half an hour the next. Risotto was clearly the answer, and foraging in the cupboard I found a can of artichoke hearts (which I drained and mashed up with a wooden spoon); a can of tomatoes (to which I did the same thing); and a can of white beans (which I drained, rinsed, and didn't mash). I stirred all these into the risotto, and it was a fine supper. In short, if you can master the technique (and you *can*), you can go pretty much anywhere with it. Also, leftover risotto (add a couple tablespoons of water to reheat it) is nothing to scoff at. You can freeze it, too.

Some other variations on a basic risotto:

• leftover asparagus, chopped, and chopped prosciutto;

• flaked fresh salmon, frozen peas, and fresh chives;

• canned pureed pumpkin (to taste) and sage;

• bay scallops, canned tomatoes, and canned white beans;

• black or white truffles (wildly expensive! and they traditionally come packed in arborio rice, to impart to the rice the flavor of truffles) with cream and Parmesan;

• chopped fresh tomatoes, chopped basil, chopped black olives, toasted pine nuts, and a tiny bit of heavy cream;

• mushrooms sauéed with a little chopped garlic and a sprinkling of thyme.

This particular risotto is tangy and pink, from the saffron threads. It's light, on the one hand. On the other hand, because risotto is a dish that feels like sustenance itself, it's warm and satisfying. It violates certain rules (e.g., some cooks are adamant about not using butter or cream with a fish risotto), but since it tastes fine, who cares?

Asparagus speaks for itself, and goes well with this dish.

For the risotto

Many risotto recipes will tell you to start by sautéing the onions until they're transparent, but have you ever been able to see through an onion? Of course not. So first sauté the onion in the butter over low heat until it's wilted and opaque, 8 to 10 minutes. Then add the rice and sauté that over low heat, stirring sometimes, until the stark whiteness turns opaque as well, another 8 to 10 minutes.

Now pour in all the wine.

If you pour in the wine now, give the risotto an enthusiastic stir, and turn off the burner entirely, the rice will continue to absorb the wine—and you can hold off adding the broth and the rest of the ingredients for 2 hours or so. This jump-starts the risotto, making it cook faster when the official stirring time comes. In any case, getting this much done ahead of time, if you're so inclined, will make you feel that you have most of the meal under control; if you're having guests, you can then start the hands-on stirring as the guests settle in. If instead you feel like cooking the whole thing now, without a 2-hour respite, add the wine, leave the heat on low, and stir it a couple of times as the rice absorbs the wine. If it's your first crack at risotto, you will feel convinced that this pathetic little bit of rice will never be enough to serve six people. You will be wrong.

Once the wine is absorbed (or when you go back to it), add the saffron and the lime juice, stirring until the juice is absorbed, which won't take very long.

Now you begin adding the broth, which goes in about a ladleful at a time. (Don't open four cans at once, though, because you might only need three—risotto is an *art*, not a science.) Stir every time you add the broth, and every couple of minutes thereafter. As each ladleful of broth is drawn into the rice, you'll see that the rice seems to get bigger, sort of like The Blob in the fifties' horror movie. This is *good*.

After about 2 cans' worth of broth has been added, stirred, etc.,

1 big Spanish onion, chopped pretty fine
6 tablespoons butter
1¾ cups arborio rice
1 cup white wine
Generous pinch of saffron (the equivalent of one of those glass capsules it sometimes comes in)*
Juice of 2 limes
Three to four 10½-ounce cans low-sodium chicken broth (or homemade broth, if you happen to have some)
2 dozen medium or large shrimp (preferably fresh, but frozen will do), peeled, cut in half (if medium) or thirds (if large)
Freshly ground pepper to taste, and salt only if you really think you need it
2 tablespoons heavy cream, approximately
Fresh parsley

*You could substitute 1 tablespoon tomato paste for the saffron, which is expensive. This will change the taste a bit, giving you a slightly different dish, and it won't glow in the same way—but it will still be pink, and it will still be good.

taste the risotto. It will probably still be on the crunchy side. Open the third can, add another ladleful, stir some more. After, say, another two rounds of this, taste the risotto again. When it tastes al dente, add yet another ladle of broth, along with the shrimp. Keep stirring. Between stirs, this is a good time to grind in some pepper as well, and also to heat the bread.

When the shrimp is cooked through, and the rice is just beyond al dente—the whole thing has the texture now of tapioca pudding—add the cream and the parsley, stir it in, set on a trivet, and serve right out of the pot, passing around the hot bread.

For the asparagus

Enough asparagus for six
2 tablespoons butter
Drizzle of fresh lemon juice
(optional but nice)
Sprinkling of salt and freshly
ground pepper
Chopped parsley
(also optional but nice)

If you can, find thin, tender-looking asparagus that don't need to be peeled. Rinse them, and then cut or snap off the purplish woody ends.

To cook them in a microwave, first dry them off. Choose a microwave-safe platter and spread them as thinly as possible over it; there shouldn't be more than three asparagus piled on top of each other. (After they're cooked you can pile them any way you want.) Cook at full blast for 3 minutes, then take them out and check on them; depending on the number of asparagus and on the microwave, it could take up to 5 minutes. They're done when they've lost that fibrous quality and turned tender.

To cook them in the conventional way, cut or snap off the ends. Choose a heavy pot with a lid big enough to lay them on their sides, and bring an inch of water, to which you've added a pinch of salt, to boil in it. Lay the asparagus in the water, turn the heat down to medium, and cover. After 5 minutes, check them. With this method, you want to stop their cooking *before* they're done, because they'll be hot enough to finish cooking on their own, so try inserting a paring knife into a stalk. It shouldn't slide in easily but offer a very slight resistance. When it does, turn off the heat, and empty out all the water as quickly as you can. (You might want to pick up the asparagus in a dish towel folded over a couple of times, so that you don't get burned, and so that the asparagus gets pretty dry.) Put the asparagus back in the still-hot pan, toss it in the butter and a drizzle of lemon juice, and sprinkle it with salt, pepper (asparagus can handle a fair amount of pepper), and the chopped parsley.

Now put the lid back on. If you've used a good heavy pot, the asparagus will stay warm close to half an hour, and still be fine to serve for another half hour after that, since asparagus can be served at room temperature and is thus a hard vegetable to complain about.

Add-a-Course Notes

First course: Sizzled, Flavored Meat on Shredded Lettuce, page 181.

Dessert: Cherry Clafouti, page 196.

Sounds pretty impressive, doesn't it? It's also pretty easy.

White beans are a natural accompaniment to lamb, as is mint—all of which make this meal, however simple to prepare, fall together in a classic way, but without being as predictable as ordinary lamb with mint jelly. This way, you have more flavors.

Baby artichokes turn up in the markets much of the year; I used to see them and think, "Well, maybe some other time." In restaurants, I've had them quartered and sizzled brown, and they were all right, but in fact tasted a little prickly. With this recipe, you discard more of the outer leaves, which may seem wasteful, but it makes for a delicate-tasting side dish, actually as easy to sauté as anything else. All these recipes can easily serve more people either by your serving smaller portions or adding a little more of everything; they're flexible.

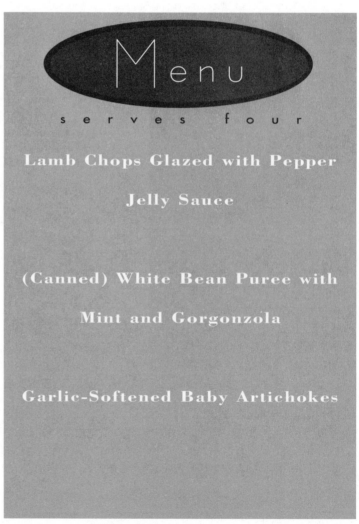

Menu

serves four

Lamb Chops Glazed with Pepper Jelly Sauce

(Canned) White Bean Puree with Mint and Gorgonzola

Garlic-Softened Baby Artichokes

For the lamb chops

Toss 4 (or however many) lamb chops in a light dressing of olive oil, balsamic vinegar, salt, and pepper—just enough to coat them lightly—then, when everything else is about ready, broil or grill them on both sides until they're done the way you like them, which I hope is pretty rare. Obviously, how long this takes varies, depending on your grill and how thick the chops are. In general, turn the first time after 3 minutes. And when they're browned on both sides, don't be afraid to cut into them to have a look inside. Contrary to myth, this doesn't make them tougher.

For the pepper jelly sauce

Put the broth and wine into a saucepan, bring to a boil, and keep going at a medium boil (you could do a high boil, but then you'd have to watch it so it wouldn't boil over) until the mixture is reduced to about ¾ cup; it doesn't have to be exact. Turn heat to low. Add the Kitchen Bouquet and spoon in the jelly a little at a time, stirring it while it melts into the broth. Taste it after you've put in nearly half the jar. You'll definitely have the pepper- jelly taste by then, but add a little more if you want it stronger.

One 10½-ounce can chicken broth, preferably Campbell's Healthy Request
½ cup wine, red or white
1 tablespoon Kitchen Bouquet
Half 8-ounce jar, give or take, of jalapeño pepper jelly, which is readily available at gourmet shops and some supermarkets

For the puree

Sauté the onion in the oil until it's wilted and opaque but not browned (if it gets a little browned, don't worry about it). Put the onion, beans, Gorgonzola, and half-and-half into a food processor and process away until you have what looks like mashed potatoes. Serve hot or warm, doesn't matter, and snip some mint into it just before you serve it, so the mint doesn't cook.

1 big Spanish onion, chopped
1 tablespoon olive oil
One 15-ounce can beans (any kind as long as they're white), rinsed and drained
2 tablespoons crumbled Gorgonzola
2 tablespoons half-and-half
Fresh mint

For the artichokes

12 baby artichokes
1 lemon
3 cloves garlic, peeled and sliced thin but not chopped
Enough olive oil to cover the bottom of a big skillet
Salt and freshly ground pepper

First, cut off the tough end of stem on the bottoms of the artichokes. If there's still some stem left, so much the better; if not, that's okay, too. Then start pulling off the leaves from the bottom and sides of the artichokes—they'll be tough—until you begin to see leaves that start to turn a tender whitish green. When you've pulled off all the outside leaves and are left with only the tender leaves, you're ready. The artichokes will each be about the size of a big mushroom. (None of this takes long. These are *baby* artichokes, after all, and small enough that you don't yet have to worry about removing the choke.)

Slice each artichoke lengthwise into four or so slices of equal width, about as wide as a chocolate dinner mint. Now squeeze the lemon juice into a bowl big enough to hold the arthchoke slices, add an inch or so of water, and toss them in the lemon water. (This is done in the hope that they won't discolor.) Now remove the artichoke slices and blot them on paper towels. Sauté the sliced garlic over low heat in enough oil to coat the bottom of a medium to large fry pan. When the garlic has softened but before it turns brown, add the artichoke slices, keeping the heat low and stirring until they're just well warmed all the way through but not brown. Remove them with a slotted spoon, if you have one, or a regular spoon if you don't, plucking out and discarding the garlic slices as you go along. Sprinkle lightly with salt and a bit of ground pepper.

Add-a-Course Notes

First course: Christopher's Smoked Fish Salad, page 173.

Dessert: Basmati Rice Pudding, page 197.

When you get right down to it, tuna fillets, which are available fresh in most places year-round, are pretty boring when grilled all by themselves. Still, they're easy, extremely good for you, and have a nice contemporary chicness to them, particularly when served on the rare side, with a pink stripe in the middle. You can also *do* things to them, like turning them into these burgers or serving them as the centerpiece to a composed main course salad, surrounded by tossed greens, string beans, tomatoes, hard-boiled eggs, red onions, and black olives. It's not cheap, tuna, but prepared this way, one pound will serve four, so in fact the per-person cost is actually fairly low. If you want, you can substitute ground chicken or turkey for the tuna, and make chicken or turkey burgers.

I suppose you could serve the burger on another kind of roll—a kaiser roll or a poppyseed roll—but it really does taste better this way, with the distinctive, crumbly texture of the corn bread getting all mixed up with the tuna and salsa. Peppers are a bore to julienne, but they go well with this meal, so it's probably worth it. The colors of the meal are yellow, red, and green; it's quite pretty.

Menu

serves four

Tuna Burgers on Corn Bread (from a Mix) with Tomato Salsa

Sautéed Peppers of Various Colors

For the corn bread

1 box corn bread mix

Mix and bake the corn bread by following the directions on the box. Two additional thoughts:

Out of laziness, I've discovered that you can actually mix the corn bread right in the baking pan (thereby precluding the need to get a mixing bowl dirty). However, the pan hasn't been greased, so you have to be more careful when you slice and remove it from the pan.

Since you're going to be serving a burger on top of the corn bread, you don't want it to be too thick. I therefore use a larger baking pan than the one called for; the burger goes right on top of the crust and you don't have to perch it on corn bread that is too high. Baking it this way reduces the cooking time, so just keep an eye on it.

For the tuna burgers

1 pound fresh tuna
(yellowfin is the best)
1 egg
4 tablespoons finely
chopped scallions,
green part only
Juice of half a lime
Generous pinch of
cayenne pepper
3 or 4 healthy dashes
hot chili sesame oil (or
as many dashes
Tabasco sauce)
Vegetable oil
1 teaspoon butter
4 to 6 quarter-size
slices fresh ginger,
unpeeled

Put the tuna in the bowl of a food processor, and pulse it until the tuna is the texture of hamburger.

Now put the tuna into a mixing bowl, add the egg, scallions, lime juice, cayenne pepper, and the hot chili sesame oil (or Tabasco). Mix well with your hands. (Removing your rings is a good idea.) Divide into four tuna burgers. It's a good idea to let them sit in the refrigerator, covered, for at least 15 minutes (they could even sit in there much longer—like all day—without harm), while you make everything else.

When it comes time to cook them, pour enough vegetable oil into a heavy skillet to barely cover the bottom, add the butter, and sauté the ginger slices over medium-high heat until they're browned on both sides. Now sauté the tuna burgers until *they're* browned on both sides; they can remain pink in the middle. The timing will vary, depending on the type of skillet and size of burgers, but start with 2 minutes on each side, or longer, until they just begin to brown. (If you're using chicken or turkey, cook them all the way through.) When it comes time to serve them, the corn bread goes on the bottom, the tuna burger on top of it, and the salsa gets spooned over both. The peppers go on the side.

For the salsa

Chop, stir everything together, and refrigerate for a little while. This recipe (useful on a host of other things, from open-faced sandwiches to chicken to, say, snapper) is, as you can probably tell, easily multiplied or divided. It keeps refrigerated only for a day or two before it begins to sag. It's best fresh.

4 tablespoons corn kernels (from a
    can is ideal, just drain it)
4 tablespoons finely chopped
    red onion
4 tablespoons finely chopped
    cucumber
4 tablespoons finely chopped tomato
1 jalapeño pepper, diced, or
    2 tablespoons from a jar
1 tablespoon white or cider vinegar
2 tablespoons vegetable oil
2 tablespoons chopped cilantro,
    added at the very end

For the peppers

Slice off the tops and bottoms of the peppers, remove the seeds, and cut the flesh into julienne strips. In a small skillet or fry pan, add enough vegetable oil to cover the bottom of the pan and sauté the garlic cloves until they're lightly browned on all sides, then throw them away unless you can think of something better to do with them.

Sauté the pepper strips all together until they're al dente,* snip on some parsley, and serve beside the tuna burgers.

1 green pepper
1 red pepper
1 yellow pepper
    (or any combination thereof)
Vegetable oil
2 cloves garlic, peeled but left whole
Parsley

Add-a-Course Notes

First course: Seasonal Remoulade, page 182.
Dessert: Sweetened Ricotta and Mixed Fruit, page 191.

*Julienned strips of pepper can also be sautéed this way in olive oil. Because this is a vegetable-oil kind of meal, there's no reason to intrude the heavier taste of olive oil, which would mix the tastes up too much. (If you're making an olive-oil type of meal and want to serve sautéed peppers, by all means use olive oil.)

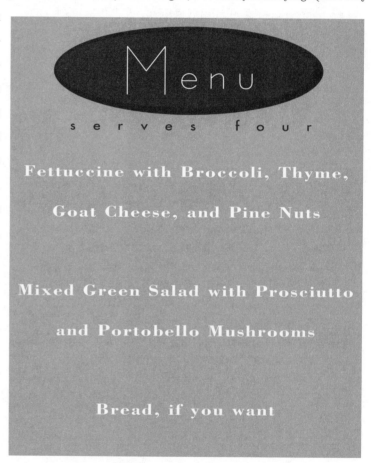

This pasta recipe is an easy knockoff of a famous chef's, and has served me (and various friends who have asked for the recipe) well for years, with its many tastes and textures. Because it's whisked into a chicken stock-based reduction, the goat cheese actually tastes light, not heavy or cloying. (The tiny bit of half-and-half or cream smooths out the sauce, which otherwise would have a slight, but noticeable, grittiness to it.) The broccoli and toasted pine nuts have subtly different textures that go really well together. It's a pity to use only the florets of the broccoli, but the dish tastes better and is prettier that way. You can make an easy soup of the stalks, or use them in another way if you can think of one.

This is a pasta dish, too, that you can vary. I've used chopped walnuts when I don't have any pine nuts; made it with fresh basil instead of thyme (stir in the chopped basil at the very end, though, just as you're serving it, not early on as you do with the thyme); and added chopped, cooked chicken breast if I have some left over. I once tried adding some minced prosciutto, but combined with the goat cheese it tasted too salty, and anyway made the dish needlessly expensive. Better, if you want a touch of meat with the meal, to set the prosciutto off in the salad. Peppery arugula is great served with Portobello mushrooms and prosciutto in this way.

Menu

serves four

Fettuccine with Broccoli, Thyme, Goat Cheese, and Pine Nuts

Mixed Green Salad with Prosciutto and Portobello Mushrooms

Bread, if you want

For the pasta

Cover the bottom of a big heavy fry pan generously with olive oil and sauté the minced shallots until they're translucent; remove from the heat before their edges begin to turn brown. Now slide the leaves from the stems of thyme—the more thyme the better—and add the leaves to the oil, discarding the stems. Add the wine and chicken broth. This is a good time, too, while you think of it, to grind in some black pepper, 1 tablespoon, give or take. (No salt, though; the goat cheese will provide salt enough.) Bring to a boil, and boil away until the mixture is reduced by about a third.

Meanwhile, put the salted pasta water on to boil and cook the broccoli florets until they're cooked through enough to get rid of that raw taste, but still crunchy. You can sauté them in a wok or skillet over high heat in a tiny bit of olive oil, or you can do them in the microwave which, if you have one, is easier—plus they'll stay a brighter green. Covered with plastic wrap, with just 3 or 4 drops of water sprinkled on top, they take 4 minutes in my microwave, but the time might vary a little with yours. Either way, cover the florets when they're cooked with a towel or plastic wrap so they'll stay warm.

Now toast the pine nuts. You can do them in a toaster oven, if you have one, using the top brown only setting; in a skillet with no oil; or on a cookie sheet placed under the broiler—whichever way seems easiest. Toast them just until they're a little bit browned (they'll begin to smell rather like popcorn at this point), swish them around a bit with a wooden spoon, and toast a little bit more, so that the newly exposed sides also get toasted. Put them to the side when they're done; it doesn't matter if they cool.

Once the broth is reduced, turn the heat to low and use a whisk to fold in the goat cheese. You can start cooking the fettuccine about now, too. When the cheese is all folded in, add the half-and-half or heavy cream. If the oil seems to separate from the cheese, just whisk a little harder. The finished sauce should be creamy and thick enough to pour, but not runny. If it's too thick, add a little water; if it's not thick enough, boil it down a little more (this won't hurt the goat cheese). How to tell? Taste it. And add more pepper if it needs it.

Olive oil
2 shallots, minced
10 or more stems fresh thyme
½ cup white wine
One 10½-ounce can chicken broth
Freshly ground pepper
4 stalks' worth broccoli florets
4 to 6 tablespoons pine nuts
Two 3-ounce logs goat cheese
2 tablespoons half-and-half or heavy cream
1 pound fettuccine

Toss the cooked and drained pasta right into the fry pan with the sauce, turning the heat up for a minute to make sure it's really hot when it gets to the table. Distribute the broccoli florets on top, working them into the pasta itself a little, to be sure they get the benefit of a little of the sauce. Sprinkle the pine nuts on top of that, take the pan right to the table, and serve.

For the salad

4 big Portobello mushrooms
4 slices prosciutto, sliced
thin with fat removed
Olive oil
Balsamic vinegar
Freshly ground pepper
1 big or 2 small bunches
arugula

First remove and discard the mushroom stems and douse the caps with olive oil and a few drops of balsamic vinegar, just enough to enable the oil to soak in well and tenderize the mushrooms. Grind some pepper onto both sides. Let them soak at least 5 minutes before grilling or broiling on both sides until they're cooked through. The time this takes will vary, depending on how thick the mushrooms are, but you want them charred-looking on both sides.

Clean the arugula well (it tends to be sandy), sprinkle lightly with olive oil, a drizzle of balsamic vinegar, and a few grindings of pepper. (The prosciutto should provide enough salt.) Divide the dressed arugula among four plates, lay the prosciutto on top and the mushroom on top of that, and serve.

Add-a-Course Notes

First course: Bruschetta with Red, Yellow, and Green Peppers page 175.
Dessert: Mix-and-Match Strawberry Sauce, page 193.

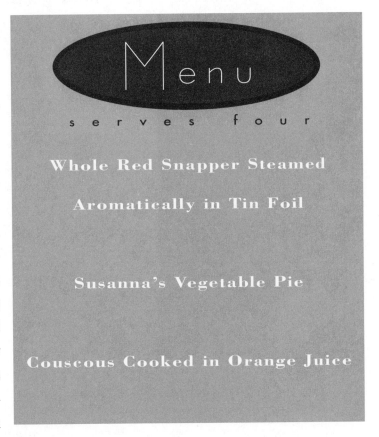

here's nothing more dramatic than presenting a whole cooked fish on a platter. Cooking one is also an intimidating thought if you've never done it: What about the head and tail? The bones? The skin? How do you cook it? How do you get it from pot to platter to plate?

With red snapper, a tasty, delicate fish available much of the year, it's easier than you'd think. With the fish right there in front of you, in fact, it's much less daunting than it is sitting in ice at the fishmonger's. In the first place, the head and tail don't get in the way. You just cut around them. You don't need fancy filleting equipment; a blunt knife and a spatula, the kind you use for flipping grilled-cheese sandwiches, are all you need. There aren't too many bones, either, and the skeleton is easily found and and easily removed, so you don't have to eat in tiny little bites, worried that you'll get surprise bones with every taste. As for the skin, you can eat it or not, but most people eat it because it blends into the fish as it's cooked and tastes fine.

Menu

serves four

Whole Red Snapper Steamed Aromatically in Tin Foil

Susanna's Vegetable Pie

Couscous Cooked in Orange Juice

When you're buying the fish, ask the fishmonger to clean it but not fillet it. He will think this request perfectly normal.

This method of cooking it uses tin foil instead of a pan, so the fish steams in aromatic vegetables, wine, and a little white vinegar (a sort of court bouillon). The vegetables also adorn the platter, but they're just for show; you don't eat them.

Vegetable pie is a different (and pretty and tasty) way of organizing eggplant and tomatoes. It holds together the same way lasagna does, and you cut it into wedges (or squares, if you're using a square or rectangular casserole) just as you would a pie.

Couscous (rhymes with moose-moose) is a Moroccan pasta sold by the box near the rice section in most supermarkets, and it's literally foolproof. (You stir the couscous into boiling water, remove from heat, and it's done in five minutes; the instructions on the box will tell you the same thing.) I'd always found it pretty bland, however, until I substituted freshly squeezed orange juice for the water one night on a whim. It absorbed the flavor readily and the combination adds a nice fruit tinge to this dinner, and others. I also plan to try tomato juice, apple juice, peach nectar, but haven't gotten around to it yet.

For the snapper

Put the onion, carrots, celery, and—if you're using them—the ginger and fennel in a Pyrex dish if you have a microwave, or any oven-worthy pot or pan if you don't. Drizzle the olive oil and vinegar over the top, pour in the wine, sprinkle on salt, grind in some pepper, and stir it a little. If you have a microwave, cover the Pyrex dish in plastic wrap, and zap it for about 15 minutes. If you don't have a microwave, bake it at 350°F for half an hour, covered in tin foil.

When the vegetables are cool, place the whole snapper on enough tin foil—it'll probably take two big sheets, overlapping lengthwise—to enclose it like a package. You'll see a hole (like the cavity of a turkey, where the stuffing goes) in the belly, from which the entrails were removed when the fish was cleaned. Fill this with the cooked vegetables and tuck the extra vegetables under the fish. Drizzle the liquid over the top, and wrap the snapper tightly in the tin foil.

Bake at 350°F, or cook it on a gas grill, for half an hour. Open the packet carefully, as it will release steam, and cut into the flesh to make sure it's cooked all the way through.

To serve, ease it onto a platter, with the vegetables around it and any remaining juice poured over the top. Loosen the flesh gently above the skeleton with a blunt knife, beginning at the top of the cavity—the spine—and lifting it off with a spatula when you get a good-size piece of it. Continue this way all along the top of the fish. Then put the knife under the skeleton, pull it up with your fingers (it will come up in one piece), discard, and continue serving the bottom half of the fish.

1 Spanish onion, coarsely chopped

2 carrots, coarsely chopped

2 stalks celery, coarsely chopped

Small knob fresh ginger, sliced but not peeled (optional)

1 head fennel, coarsely chopped (optional)

2 tablespoons white vinegar

6 tablespoons olive oil

1 cup dry white wine

Salt and freshly ground black pepper

1 whole red snapper, about 5 pounds, cleaned but not filleted

4 lemon wedges, to garnish the platter

For the vegetable pie

2 medium eggplants
Salt
⅓ cup flour
2 to 3 big tomatoes
3 eggs
⅓ cup grated
Parmesan cheese
2 tablespoons chopped
fresh parsley or basil (or
both)
Freshly ground pepper
1 cup (about 6 ounces)
grated Monterey Jack or
cheddar cheese, or a
mixture of both

Preheat the oven to 350°F. Slice the egglants about as thick as an Oreo cookie. Lay the slices flat on dishtowels or paper towels and sprinkle lightly with salt to help release the water. Leave them for about 15 minutes, pat the tops dry, sprinkle lightly and as evenly as possible with the flour (dredging, it's called), and put them in the oven for 10 minutes on a cookie sheet (you'll probably have to do two batches). When they are cool enough to handle, which will take about 10 seconds, raise the oven temperature to 400° and start making the pie.

In a pie dish, casserole (about the same size), or oven-worthy skillet, cover the bottom with a layer of the eggplant slices; no oil is necessary. Slice the tomatoes to about the same thickness, then cover the eggplant layer with tomato slices, then eggplant slices, then tomato slices, and so on until all the slices are gone.

Whisk together the eggs, Parmesan cheese, herbs, a couple of sprinkles of salt, and several generous grindings of pepper until they're all blended, and pour this mixture over the pie. Now sprinkle the Monterey Jack or cheddar cheese on top, and bake at 400° for 20 minutes. (This can be cooked ahead of time, covered in tin foil to keep it warm, and reheated, or put under the broiler for a couple of minutes.) Let it sit 5 or 10 minutes to firm up before serving.

For the couscous

Follow the package directions, substituting orange juice (freshly squeezed is vastly better here than bottled) for the water. If you have any parsley around, or a bit of chopped red pepper, you can garnish it with one or both, but there's certainly no real need to.

Add-a-Course Notes

First course: Pizza, page 179.

Dessert: Pear Crisp, page 195.

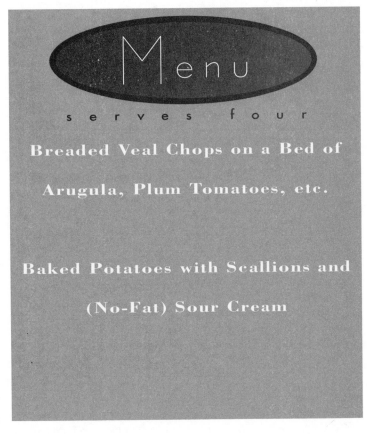

or years, I'd order veal chops in restaurants and never cook them at home because I thought there was somthing mysterious about them. There's nothing mysterious about them at all, as it turns out. They're expensive, so I make them only occasionally and usually just for dinners à deux. But they're easy.

Often they are served dressed on a salad this way at good bistros; the presentation is very pretty and clean, with the salad served fluffed around the veal chop. You can also grill or broil them the same way, and serve them with a warmed or room-temperature store-bought marinara sauce to pour over them instead of the salad (but if you do, you'll be required to come up with something green to put on the plate). Some people sauté them, which is fine, but they're lighter if you grill or broil them.

As for baked potato, it's satisfying and filling, and makes this elegantly simple meal complete. Chopping as many scallions—radishes and scallions together are a nice variation—into the (no-fat) sour cream as will fit gives it more spirit, crunch, and taste, enough so that most diners won't need butter or salt—just a pepper mill.

The butcher will pound the veal chops to any thickness you want, but it's useful to know how to do it yourself as well, in case you're ever pounding them on a desert island. The meat pounder looks like a hammer, with two sides to the head. The flat side is for pounding meat, to make it an even thick-

Menu

serves four

Breaded Veal Chops on a Bed of Arugula, Plum Tomatoes, etc.

Baked Potatoes with Scallions and (No-Fat) Sour Cream

ness for cooking and pretty to present. The scored side with the pyramidal points is for tenderizing tough cuts of meat (e.g., beef for cube steaks); the points break up tough connective tissue, making it easier and more palatable to chew. Veal chops are tender to begin with, so here you'd use the flat side only, and pound them, between sheets of wax paper, to increase their size by half, not so much so that they end up paper thin. You could also try flattening them with a rolling pin or pounding with the blade of a cleaver.

For the veal chops

1 egg
½ cup milk (low fat or otherwise)
1 tablespoon plus 1 teaspoon Dijon mustard
4 veal chops, pounded as described above
2 cups herbed (or plain) bread crumbs

Whisk together the egg, milk, and mustard in a bowl big enough to accommodate the veal chops, and give each chop a good soak, immersing it for 20 seconds or so. Put the bread crumbs in another bowl big enough to accommodate the chops and dip them in to coat thoroughly, shaking off any excess. Put the breaded chops between layers of wax paper into the refrigerator for half an hour, or in the freezer for 15 minutes, to help the crumbs adhere.

Just before serving (they should come to the table really hot), broil or grill for 3 minutes on each side, then cut into the middle of one to see how they're doing. All the pink should disappear, and they should be whitish all the way through.

For the salad

1 to 2 bunches arugula, cleaned well
1 red onion, peeled, cut in half, and sliced into C-shaped rings
8 plum tomatoes, eached chopped (not sliced) into 4 or 6 pieces
2 handfuls black olives, preferably Moroccan, pitted or not

For the vinaigrette

First make the vinaigrette by whisking all the ingredients together well. Put the onions into the vinaigrette to marinate, stirring to cover them well. Marinating them for as little as 15 minutes will take the raw edge off, and also impart more flavor to the vinaigrette itself. (Marinating them longer is fine, too.) When it's time for dinner, toss the rest of the salad together, fluff it up around the veal chops, and serve the potatoes on the side.

½ cup olive oil
2 tablespoons balsamic
   vinegar
2 teaspoons dry mustard
Salt and freshly ground
   pepper

For the baked potatoes

Rinse the potatoes, prick them about three times each with a fork, and bake at 350°F for 45 minutes to an hour, depending on their size. To tell when they're done, when pinched the very top of the skin should feel as if there's a little air between the skin and the pulp of the potato. When the water bakes out, the skin begins to get crispy and the pulp begins to separate from the skin on top and sink toward the bottom. They're done when that happens.

Chop the scallions, green parts and all, and mix into the sour cream, so that it's replete with scallions. Either cut into the potatoes yourself and add a dollop of sour cream to each potato, or serve the sour cream on the side. (The former is prettier.)

4 baking potatoes
1 bunch scallions
1 cup low-fat sour cream

Add-a-Course Notes

First course: Seafood Salad, page 171.

Dessert: Suzanne's Blueberry (Cake Mix) Cobbler, page 188.

 At a pricey restaurant once, my husband, Michael, ordered a pasta with a fancy name that turned out to be rigatoni with sausage in a creamy tomato sauce. When it came, it was delicious, like gourmet baby food for grown-ups, if that makes sense. It struck me as awfully expensive, though, for what it seemed to be, which was a simple sauce made with cheap ingredients. It struck me, too, that I could figure out how to make it at home.

There was a full-bodiedness to it that suggested that the chef had used a reduction of liquor—red wine perhaps?—when boiling down the tomatoes. I didn't want to use wine myself, however, because both tomatoes and wines are acidic, and the combination seemed too much. Vodka, which I'd seen listed as an ingredient in other tomato sauces, seemed right, and it was. The sauce *was* utterly simple to re-create, and in a way I'm sorry I learned it, because Michael has never treated me to dinner at that restaurant again. The recipe, by the way, can easily be doubled, or quintupled, for that matter, and I usually double it to freeze some. Garnishing the dish with a few basil leaves and black olives on the side is a nice touch, if you happen to have basil leaves and black olives lying around; otherwise I wouldn't bother.

Menu

serves four

Rigatoni with Pink Sauce

Green Salad with Pears and Shaved Parmesan

Bread, if you want

Because Parmesan cheese does nothing to help this sauce, put it on the salad instead. Shaved Parmesan on top of salads is a touch you sometimes see in restaurants, but it can be done at home, too, with a wide-bladed vegetable peeler. You just shave it as if you were peeling a potato. It doesn't matter if the shavings all come out the same size (they probably won't!); just place them over the lettuce and pears in a lattice fashion without apology.

For the pasta

First, deal with the sausages. Prick the casings in a number of places with a fork, so as to let the fat drain out. To cook them conventionally, sauté in a tiny bit of vegetable oil, enough so that they don't stick, until they're browned and cooked all the way through, 10 minutes or so. If you have a microwave, put them in a microwave-safe pan (or on a plate) with two paper towels underneath and two on top. In my microwave, they take about 8 minutes, give or take. They may not brown very well, but it doesn't matter, as you're going to put them into the food processor anyway.

Sauté the onion and garlic in the vegetable oil in a good-size fry pan until they're both softened but not browned. Add the vodka and tomatoes and boil away for about 20 minutes until the liquid is reduced and you're left with a big mess of tomatoey glop. (You won't want to boil at your stove's highest heat, or tomato will get all over the wall—a rolling bubble is more like it.)

If you're going to be serving dinner right away, this is a good time to put salted water on to boil for the rigatoni.

Put the sausages into a food processor and pulse until they're the texture of hamburger, then take them out and put them somewhere. Now put the tomato glop into the food processor and pulse that, too, until the mixture is smooth. Put it back into the pan and stir in the chopped-up sausage. Now add the half-and-half a little at a time, as you keep stirring. The mixture will begin to turn pink, which is what you want. The texture should not be runny but have some body to it, so that it really adheres to the pasta. It varies a little each time, but 1/2 to 3/4 cup half-and-half, give or take a little, ought to do it. Keep it hot. Add salt and freshly ground pepper to taste, toss together with the rigatoni, and serve, garnished with basil leaves and black olives, if desired.

4 hot Italian sausages

1 big Spanish onion, coarsely chopped

4 cloves garlic, peeled and cut into 2 or 3 pieces

2 tablespoons vegetable oil

1/3 cup vodka

1 28-ounce can crushed tomatoes

3/4 cup half-and-half, approximately

Salt and freshly ground pepper

1 pound rigatoni or other short pasta such as penne or radiatore

Basil leaves and black olives, for garnish (optional)

For the salad

Wedge of Parmesan, the size of a piece of pie, for shaving
1 big head green or red leaf lettuce
2 big pears, cored and slivered at the last minute

For the vinaigrette

⅓ cup olive oil
1 tablespoon plus 1 tea-
spoon red wine vinegar
(or white wine, or balsamic)
1 teaspoon dry mustard
Salt and freshly
ground pepper

Shave the Parmesan, putting it somewhere so that it's handy when you're ready to arrange it. Clean the lettuce, leaving the leaves whole, if possible, rather than chopping or shredding to bits. Set them on a platter or in a bowl. When you're ready to serve the salad, slice the pears, toss the lettuce in the vinaigrette, lay the pears on top, and the Parmesan on top of that—so that when you present it, you mostly see Parmesan slivers with just a little lettuce and pear peeking out from underneath.

Add-a-Course Notes

First course: Smoked Salmon with Dilled Honey-Mustard Sauce, page 177.

Dessert: Peter's Chocolate Cake, page 194.

*W*hoever even thinks about duck breasts? No one, and that's the beauty of it. You can probably have the monopoly in your neighborhood and, with this meal alone, people will think you're a wonderful and exotic cook. If you've never had them, you'll surely like them if you like chicken breasts. The taste is similar, but deeper somehow.

Duck breasts are one of the best kept secrets in the world of cooking: delicious, thoroughly easy to work with, definitely gourmet, and not at all full of fat and mystery. Somewhere in the back of the meat locker, many butchers keep an ongoing supply of duck breasts, which come frozen and shrink-wrapped in plastic in bags of six or eight. If a butcher doesn't have them on hand, he'll know what you mean when you ask for them and be able to order them easily. It's worth checking a few days ahead to be sure, and if you want them for, say, a Saturday, he'll have them out of the freezer for you. They're more expensive than chicken, but cheaper than serving a good steak.

Menu

s e r v e s   s i x

Composed Duck Breast Salad

on a Bed of Polenta

Faux Fresh Applesauce

It's true that most ducks grown for commercial use have a lot of fat under the skin, which drains away during cooking; the breasts themselves are lean. For this reason the ideal way to cook them is on an outdoor grill: They'll splatter a lot when exposed to the hot flame, but they cook in as little as five minutes. An alternative method is to sauté them in a little olive oil in a preheated cast-iron skillet on high. Once the fat has drained away, they're lean as can be. If a little fat remains, you can easily peel away the skin, but most cooks usually leave it right where it is.

If you have a big platter, this dish is unusually pretty to serve. The duck breasts are cooked, preferably rare to medium rare, sliced thin, and laid on a bed of polenta, a gourmet version of cornmeal mush that comes in a box. Then the sauce, hot and earthy with the essence of dried mushrooms, is poured over the duck and works its way into the polenta, too. The salad—mostly from cans and the freezer—is tossed in a vinaigrette and spread around the duck-polenta. Very dramatic. Alternatively, you can serve the duck and polenta on one platter, the salad on another or in a bowl, and compose the salad right on the dinner plates. Whichever seems easier.

The applesauce is just an extra touch, and it should be served from a separate bowl, not mixed up with the salad.

For the duck breasts

6 duck breasts
(they'll come boned)

Prick the skin side of the duck breasts six or eight times with a fork, as if they were potatoes to be baked but more so. (Don't marinate them; the fat keeps them really tender.) If cooking on a grill, place them skin side down, and use a long fork to push them around.

Turn them over after about 3 minutes, and cut into the middle of one to check their progress after 5 minutes. If using a skillet, cover the bottom in a thin coat of olive oil, preheat on high until the oil is really hot, and sauté the breasts meat side down for 3 minutes, reduce the heat, then turn and cook the breasts skin side down for another 3. Rare to medium rare is the way most people like them.

You can cook them ahead of time, if you're so inclined; they can be served at room temperature with the hot sauce poured over. To serve, pull off or cut away the skin if you want to, and slice thin and prettily, on the diagonal.

For the sauce

In a saucepan big enough to hold all these ingredients, sauté the shallots in the butter until they're wilted. Add the broth, wine, vinegar, and mushrooms and bring to a boil. Boil until the mixture is reduced to about ¾ cup. Put it through a strainer to get rid of the mushrooms and shallots, then put it back into the saucepan over low heat, add the Gravy Master, grind in some black pepper, and stir in the chives. Serve it hot, drizzled over the duck.

2 shallots, coarsely chopped
1 tablespoon butter
One 10½-ounce can chicken broth
¾ cup red wine
½ teaspoon balsamic vinegar
3 tablespoons dried mushrooms, any kind, broken into bits
1 tablespoon Gravy Master
Freshly ground pepper
3 tablespoons finely chopped fresh chives or parsley

For the polenta

The box of polenta in my cupboard says that it makes approximately five servings—but it's more than enough for six. Follow the package directions, don't try to cheat on the stirring, and stir in the half-and-half at the end, which will make it creamier. Just before serving and while still hot, make a bed of it, lay the slices of duck on top, and pour the hot sauce over the duck.

1 box polenta
½ cup half-and-half

For the salad

One 15¼-ounce can corn, drained and rinsed
One 10-ounce box frozen lima beans, simmered as directed until al dente
One 15-ounce can small white beans, drained and rinsed
1 green (or red or yellow) pepper, finely chopped
1 bunch scallions, both white and green parts, finely chopped
6 tablespoons finely chopped basil (or dill, cilantro, or parsley)

For the vinaigrette

⅔ cup olive oil
3 tablespoons balsamic
vinegar
1 tablespoon plus
1 teaspoon dry mustard
Salt and freshly
ground pepper

Mix together all the ingredients for the salad except the herbs. In a separate bowl, whisk together the ingredients for the vinaigrette.

Toss the salad with the vinaigrette and chill in the refrigerator if you have time, to enable the flavors to blend. This will even keep overnight, covered. Bring back to room temperature before serving, and toss again at the last minute with the herbs.

For the applesauce

2 apples or pears
1 tablespoon butter
Generous pinch cinnamon
One 16-ounce jar of
applesauce

Peel the apples or pears and cut into small chunks. Sauté gently in the butter until they're soft, adding the cinnamon toward the end.

Stir in the applesauce and serve.

To assemble: One way or another, each dinner plate should end up with several slices of duck breast on top of some polenta, surrounded by a ring of the salad, with a little applesauce on the side.

Add-a-Course Notes

First course: Linguine with Rosemary-Gorgonzola Sauce, page 167.

Dessert: Demitasse Chocolate, page 192.

$\mathcal{I}$t will seem at first glance that these crab cakes require a lot of work, but most of it is just a lot of chopping and mixing and paying attention at the beginning. It's true, too, that you have to make them enough in advance to chill the mix thoroughly before you actually form the cakes and fry them—so they're a dish to save for the weekend. Crabmeat is expensive, relatively, but if you think of the cost of feeding six people crab cakes, it's probably cheaper than ordering crab cakes for two at a good restaurant. One pound of crabmeat will make six big enough or twelve smallish crab cakes: That stretches fairly well.

Crabmeat comes in one-pound vacuum-packed tins that need to be kept cold; most fish shops carry it year-round. They might do it automatically, but if not, ask them to open the can and pick through the crabmeat to remove any remaining cartilage.

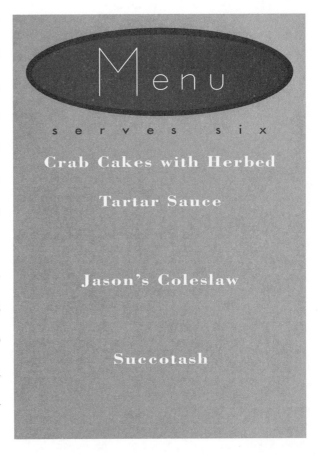

Menu

serves six

Crab Cakes with Herbed

Tartar Sauce

Jason's Coleslaw

Succotash

The coleslaw gets better after it's been chilled, too, so if you're serving this meal to guests, the main thrust of work should probably take place in the morning or early afternoon, after which you can take the afternoon off. (The succotash is very little trouble.)

For the crab-cake mix

3 cloves garlic, finely chopped
3 tablespoons finely chopped onion
1 small red pepper, finely chopped
2 tablespoons butter
3 tablespoons flour
2/3 cup heavy cream
2 teaspoons dry mustard
2 teaspoons Dijon mustard
4 tablespoons finely chopped mixed (choose two or, better, three)
    fresh herbs—basil, chives, parsley, cilantro, tarragon
Juice of 1 lemon
1/2 teaspoon cayenne pepper
Few dashes of Tabasco or hot sauce
2 egg yolks
1/2 cup bread crumbs
1 pound crabmeat, picked through to remove any cartilage

To fry the crab cakes

1 egg
1 cup milk
1 1/2 cups bread crumbs
Vegetable oil

In a big, heavy fry pan, sauté the garlic, onion, and pepper gently in the butter until the onion wilts. Keeping the heat at medium to medium low, stir in the flour and continue to stir constantly for a minute or two until it's well incorporated into the butter. Add the cream and, again, keep stirring for another minute or two as it thickens. (The flour-butter step is the only tricky part, and it's only mildly tricky: We're only talking about stirring for at most 4 minutes.) Now add the mustards, herbs, lemon juice, cayenne pepper, Tabasco, and egg yolks. Stir well, remove from the heat, and mix in the 1/2 cup bread crumbs and the crabmeat, using your hands if it's easier. Refrigerate for at least 3 hours (or freeze for an hour and refrigerate for another hour).

When it comes time to cook the crab cakes, whisk the egg and milk together in a bowl, and put the 1½ cups bread crumbs into a second bowl. Shape all the crab cakes first (to make sure they're the same size), dip each one into the egg-milk mixture, then coat with bread crumbs. Heat enough vegetable oil to cover the bottom of a heavy fry pan or skillet, then sauté each cake on both sides in the sizzling oil. Serve with herbed tartar sauce, or even just a lemon wedge.

For the herbed tartar sauce

Mix together well, and serve with the crab cakes.

¼ cup sour cream (no fat is fine)
½ cup mayonnaise (low fat is fine)
¼ cup Dijon mustard
2 tablespoons ketchup or chili sauce
1 teaspoon white or cider vinegar
Dash of Tabasco or hot sauce
2 cornichons, finely chopped, or 1 table-spoon pickle relish
1 hard-boiled egg, finely chopped
2 tablespoons finely chopped mixed fresh herbs (use leftovers from the crab cakes)

For the coleslaw

Two tricks here. One is that the cabbage, onion, and pepper have to be sliced or shredded fine—a vegetable slicer or mandoline will do this in no time. The second is that as the cabbage is shredded, it seems to pile up in the bowl and look like more than anyone could possibly need. Don't worry about this: The dressing will be poured over it hot, and the cabbage will deflate to the right amount.

Shred or slice the cabbage, onion, and green pepper. In a small saucepan, bring the oil, vinegar, and sugar to a boil, and boil gently until the sugar melts. Whisk a

1 small head green cabbage
1 big Spanish onion
1 green pepper, cored and seeds removed
⅓ cup vegetable oil
¾ cup white or cider vinegar
½ cup sugar
1 teaspoon caraway seeds
1 teaspoon celery seeds
Salt and freshly ground pepper

couple of times, and pour the hot dressing over the cabbage, onion, and pepper. Add caraway seeds, celery seeds, a little salt, and some freshly ground pepper. Mix well, and chill if possible before serving.

For the succotash

2 tablespoons butter
1 small Spanish onion, finely chopped
One 10-ounce box frozen lima beans
One 10-ounce box frozen corn
2 to 3 tablespoons heavy cream
3 tablespoons finely chopped parsley
Dash Tabasco sauce
Salt and freshly ground pepper
Paprika

Sauté the onion in the butter until it wilts. Stir in the lima beans, corn, and heavy cream, and heat through. Add the parsley, a dash of Tabasco, and salt and pepper to taste, then sprinkle with paprika and serve.

Add-a-Course Notes

First course: Ham Mousse with Melon, page 170.

Dessert: Peter's Chocolate Cake, page 194.

alk low fat all you want, but aren't there times when you just want a steak? A real steak? With all the things that you can order with it at a really good steakhouse? The best way to eat steak is, in fact, at such an establishment, where you can watch all the steaks and fried things going by as you wait for ... nd best way is to make it yourself, although it won't be

Menu

serves four

Steakhouse Pepper Steak

Potato Chips

Creamed Spinach

Chopped Salad

...inese cooking. "But all that oil," you say. "Doesn't it get ... filter work fine) back into the bottle, and use it again the next time you deep-fry. It's also a good idea at least to slice the potatoes a couple of hours ahead of when you plan to use them, since they need to soak in ice water to release their starch.

You can tone down any of the elements here you like: Broil the steak simply, instead of making pepper steak; baked potatoes instead of chips; plain old spinach instead of creamed; and a different salad—but for some reason all these ingredients taste quite good and feel like steakhouse fare when chopped fine and tossed together.

For the pepper steak

4 tablespoons peppercorns
4 pieces strip sirloin steak, not too thick (1 inch is thick enough), trimmed of fat and with any bones removed
½ cup butter
Juice of 1 lemon
2 tablespoons A.1. sauce
Dash or two of Worcestershire sauce
2 tablespoons finely chopped parsley
1 tablespoon salt

Put the peppercorns between two layers of wax paper, and roll with a rolling pin (or wine bottle, meat pounder, or whatever you can find) to break up the peppercorns into coarse fragments, but larger than if you were grinding it through a grinder. Dip the steaks—both sides—into the pepper, pressing hard with your hand in the hope that the pepper will pretty much stick to the steak.

Melt the butter somehow, and whisk together with the lemon juice, A.1. sauce, Worcestershire, and parsley. Keep this handy.

Sprinkle the bottom of a cast-iron (or other heavy) skillet with the salt, or half the salt if the steaks will have to be cooked in two batches. Set the heat to high and heat the skillet until it's hot, reduce the heat to medium, and immediately put in the steaks, flipping them quickly to seal, then flipping back to cook. Cook for a couple of minutes on each side, then cut into the steaks to check for doneness. When they're about right, pour in the butter mixture (or half of it, if you're doing two batches), flip them quickly to leave a trace of it on both sides. The steaks shouldn't be *doused* in the sauce, just glazed with it.

For the potato chips

Don't peel the potatoes, but cut off any ends too small for making chips. Using a vegetable slicer or mandoline, slice the potatoes thin, put them into a bowl of ice water, and refrigerate. Replace the ice water with new ice water from time to time. You'll actually see the starch leaching out, and the potatoes will begin to seize and get crispier, just from the water. Very important: After a couple of hours, dry the potatoes well—patting them with bath towels is the best way.

4 to 6 big baking potatoes
Vegetable oil for frying
Salt, preferably kosher salt

As you begin to dry the potatoes thoroughly, which will take a while, pour the oil into the pan (about halfway up the sides) and begin to heat it on low heat; as it warms, keep turning up the heat little by little. If you have a frying thermometer (don't use any other kind of thermometer), you want to get the heat up to 375°F. If you don't have a frying thermometer, get the oil hot—but not to the point where it's smoking. Put a drop of water in to test; when it sizzles, try a potato slice. When the oil is hot enough, the potato will begin to sizzle and fry right away. This is a good time, too, to tear up some brown paper bags into sheets for draining the potatoes. (Or you can use paper towels, but bags are better.)

Drop a handful of potato slices in and watch carefully. Hot fat can overflow, which is why a frying basket is great: You can just lift it out, and lower it back in and it'll be fine. Otherwise, using pot holders, lift the pan off the heat for a minute. Stir the potatoes once or twice with the non-spoon end of a wooden spoon so they don't stick together, then just let them fry until they look like potato chips. When they do, lift them out of the oil (frying basket, slotted spoon), drain on paper bags, sprinkle lightly with salt, and keep warm in a 200°F oven. Heat the oil up for a minute before frying the next batch.

What I usually do, which makes it easy, is to put a piece of paper bag in a wooden salad bowl, then the chips, then another piece of paper bag for the next batch, then more chips—and discard each piece of paper bag before putting on the next one. A wooden salad bowl is a good thing to serve them in, and also can withstand the warm oven.

For the spinach

One 10-ounce package fresh spinach or one 10-ounce box frozen
3 tablespoons finely chopped Spanish onion
2 tablespoons butter
1 tablespoon flour
⅓ cup heavy cream
3 tablespoons finely chopped parsley
Salt, freshly ground pepper, and freshly ground nutmeg

If you're using fresh spinach, pull off any browned bits or curled-up stems, rinse, shake off excess water, and cook just until wilted with the water that remains on it. When cool, wring it out to get rid of excess water, and chop very fine. If using frozen, just let it defrost, wring out, and chop fine.

In any kind of pan except cast iron (which reacts badly to the iron in spinach, or so I'm told), sauté the onion in the butter, then, over low heat, stir in the flour till it's well incorporated, then add the cream in a drizzle, stirring as you do. When the mixture is smooth, toss in the spinach, parsley, a little salt, and a few grindings each of pepper and nutmeg. Serve as soon as it gets hot.

For the chopped salad

1 bunch radishes, sliced, with each slice quartered
1 cucumber, peeled and sliced, with each slice quartered
1 bunch scallions (or a red or white onion), chopped into bits the same size as above
1 tomato, chopped into small bits
1 small head romaine or iceberg lettuce, chopped
2 tablespoons finely chopped parsley
Optional: chopped hard-boiled egg; chopped leftover string beans; bits of chopped, cooked bacon or shrimp; anything else that seems right

Toss together with a simple red or white wine vinaigrette whisked together, such as:

⅓ cup olive oil
1½ to 2 tablespoons red or white wine vinegar
1 teaspoon dry mustard
Salt and freshly ground pepper to taste

Add-a-Course Notes

First course: Smoked Salmon with Dilled Honey-Mustard Sauce, page 177.
Dessert: Apple Tart, page 189.

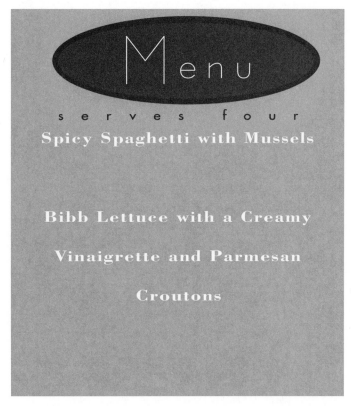

paghetti or linguine with clam sauce has by now achieved the status of a classic, whereas spaghetti (or linguine) with mussels sounds a little more exotic—and is actually easier and very quick to make. It's light and clean-tasting—a perfect supper dish. It could also be made as a first course to a more complicated meal, but I like it served as the *whole* meal, with just a little light salad afterward. Adding a dollop of mayonnaise to a vinaigrette (for variety, and to make it creamy and sweet-tasting) is something I knew to do but had forgotten about, until my friend Barbara reminded me about it recently. I won't forget again. The croutons are a good counterpoint to the sweetish dressing and tie the two courses together somehow, since one doesn't put cheese on this pasta.

Menu

s e r v e s   f o u r

Spicy Spaghetti with Mussels

Bibb Lettuce with a Creamy Vinaigrette and Parmesan Croutons

I've noticed that some growers are farming huge (by mussel standards) mussels, but here the pasta is served with the mussels still in their shells so you want the tiniest ones you can find, and ones with pure black shells, not marked up. (If you can't find small ones, just leave a few in their shells to look pretty, and discard the rest of the shells, tossing the mussels back in the pasta.

Inexperienced cooks might find the ubiquitous instructions to remove the beard from the mussels a little puzzling: Do you do this with a *razor?* It's actually one of those things that's much easier to do with the mussels right in front of you than it is to think about beforehand. As they're gathered, they're eating seaweed or sea grasses. When you take them home from the fish store, they'll open their shells a little for air and with many of them you'll be able to see the bits of grass as the shells close back up when you wash them. (Or the shells will already be closed with the bits of grass sticking out.) This is the beard, and all you have to do is yank it to remove it. Sometimes you won't get it all, which is okay. As with everything else, just do your best.

For the pasta

Olive oil
3 dozen mussels, as small as possible, washed and bearded
4 cloves garlic, peeled and sliced thin (not minced)
1 fresh jalapeño pepper, stem removed, sliced thin (not minced)
1½ cups dry white wine
1 pound spaghetti
4 plum tomatoes, sliced and chopped fine
3 to 4 tablespoons finely chopped fresh basil
Freshly ground pepper

Put the water on for the pasta. Remembering that mussels double in volume as their shells open, choose a big enough pot or frying pan, one with a lid. Put in just enough olive oil to cover the bottom, add the mussels, garlic, jalapeño pepper, and wine. Cover, bring to a gentle boil, and cook until the mussels open completely. You can put the pasta in to cook while the mussels are steaming. When the mussels have opened, add the tomatoes, basil, and a few grindings of pepper, toss with the pasta, and serve.

For the salad

1 to 2 heads Bibb lettuce, depending on the size of the heads, cleaned and shredded into bite-size pieces
2 cucumbers, peeled and sliced thin

Toss the lettuce and cucumbers with the vinaigrette.

For the vinaigrette

Whisk everything together until well blended, adding ground pepper to taste.

⅓ cup olive oil
1 tablespoon balsamic vinegar
Dollop of mayonnaise (low fat is okay)
Pinch of salt
Freshly ground pepper

For the Parmesan croutons

Brush the lightly toasted slices of bread with olive oil, then rub with garlic and sprinkle on the Parmesan. Toast in a toaster oven or under the broiler until the cheese melts and begins to brown. Serve with the salad, two for each person.

8 not-very-thick slices baguette, very lightly toasted
Olive oil
2 cloves garlic, peeled and cut in half
¾ cup finely grated Parmesan cheese, approximately

Add-a-Course Notes

First course: Sizzled, Flavored Meat on Shredded Lettuce, page 181.

Dessert: Suzanne's Blueberry (Cake Mix) Cobbler, page 188.

 Lamb patties went from being a concoction I'd never heard of one day to a food that kept turning up all over the place the next. They're easy, they're lean, and they taste more grown-up than hamburgers. You could season them in any number of ways, but this way is adapted from the way I saw my friend Joe make them the first time I tasted them. I've seen ground lamb at the supermarket, but

they don't always have it; a butcher will happily grind it for you, and won't think you're strange for asking. Because lamb is leaner than most cuts of ground beef, one needs to take care that it doesn't dry out. Mixing a little oil into it when you're seasoning it and brushing it with oil once on each side when you're cooking it will help. So will making the patties small; better to serve two small juicy ones to each person than one dried-out big one. The yogurt sauce, which is served on the side, goes nicely with the Indian sensibility of the herbs.

Menu

serves six

Lamb Patties with Three Spices and Yogurt-Cucumber-Dill Dressing

Spicy Corn Pudding

There are probably a million ways to make corn pudding. The addition of jalapeño peppers to this one makes it a little spicy.

For the lamb patties

Mix all together with your hands, and shape into twelve patties. When it comes time to cook them, broil or grill, brush olive oil over them once on each side as they cook. Alternatively, you can sauté them in olive oil to cover the bottom of a cast-iron skillet over fairly high heat. Cook to medium well done, or however you like them.

2 ¾ to 3 pounds ground lamb
3 cloves garlic, finely minced
1 teaspoon ground cumin
1 teaspoon curry powder
1 teaspoon ground turmeric
1 teaspoon salt
1 teaspoon freshly ground pepper
    or more to taste
3 tablespoons olive oil, plus extra
    for brushing on the patties as
    they cook

For the yogurt sauce

Peel the cucumbers, and slice them very thin, preferably with a mandoline, or chop them fine. Salt them lightly and put them in a strainer, so as to let the water drain out, for a few minutes, pressing occasionally with paper towels to absorb the moisture. Slice the onion very thin as well. While the cucumbers are releasing their moisture, mix the yogurt, sour cream, onion, dill, Tabasco, 1 teaspoon salt, and pepper together, then stir in the cucumber. Refrigerate if you have time to let the flavors meld, and serve with the lamb patties, on the side.

2 cucumbers
Salt
Half a Spanish onion
2 cups low-fat yogurt
½ cup sour cream (no fat is fine)
4 tablespoons finely chopped dill
Dash of Tabasco sauce
Freshly ground pepper to taste

For the corn pudding

Two 15½-ounce cans corn, drained
4 tablespoons finely chopped red pepper, approximately
4 tablespoons finely chopped Spanish onion, approximately
1 fresh jalapeño pepper, finely chopped, or approximately 3 tablespoons finely chopped jalapeño pepper from a jar
3 eggs
2 tablespoons butter, melted
1 cup milk, heated with the butter until warm
Sprinkling of salt
Freshly ground pepper to taste
1 cup (6 ounces) grated Monterey Jack or mozzarella cheese to sprinkle on top (low fat is fine; optional)

Preheat the oven to 350°F, and butter a casserole or cast-iron skillet big enough to hold everything. Stir the corn, red pepper, onion, and jalapeño pepper into the casserole. Beat the eggs into the heated milk and butter, and pour over the corn mixture. Sprinkle salt and grind some pepper over the pudding, then sprinkle on the cheese, if desired. Bake until set and golden on top, about 45 minutes.

Add-a-Course Notes

First course: Christopher's Smoked Fish Salad, page 173.

Main course: Substitute Spinach with Ginger, Garlic, and Scallions (page 86) for the pudding.

Dessert: Basmati Rice Pudding, page 197.

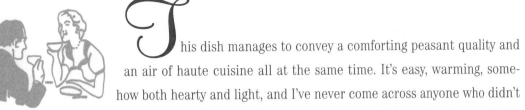

his dish manages to convey a comforting peasant quality and an air of haute cuisine all at the same time. It's easy, warming, somehow both hearty and light, and I've never come across anyone who didn't like it. Cooking it is an utterly relaxed experience; you can complete it start to finish in probably

an hour, or you can attend to the chicken, sausage, and mushrooms as far ahead as you like, and have everything that goes *into* the risotto ready to assemble before you actually start the rice itself. (If you've never made risotto before, you might want to read the pep talk about it beginning on page 94.) The recipe is easily doubled (or quadrupled, for that matter, and made in two pots for a big crowd), and easily frozen if you have any left over.

Basically the entire dish is done in four acts, made much easier if you have a microwave. You cook the chicken, the sausage, the mushrooms; then you make the risotto and stir in the already-cooked chicken, sausage, and

Menu

serves six

Earthy Risotto, Fragrant with Mushrooms

Mixed Green Salad with Marilyn's Garlic-Intense Dressing

Bread, if you want

mushrooms (along with parsley, some Parmesan, and a mere trace of heavy cream) at the end. It *sounds* complicated because of all the separate steps, but it's really pretty mindless. And the simple salad made piquant with tons of garlic (or a little less, if you're not a garlic fanatic) is a wake-up taste to follow the creamy-tasting warmth of the risotto.

This dressing uses less vinegar than the usual vinaigrette, and uses it more as a seasoning than to balance the oil; the real taste comes from the garlic, and the extra jolt from the Tabasco. You can make extra and store it in the refrigerator; it lasts until it runs out.

For the risotto

8 Italian sausages, sweet or hot
Olive oil (optional)
1 pound, give or take, skinless, boneless chicken breasts
1 ounce dried mushrooms, any kind
24 plain old supermarket mushrooms, give or take
8 tablespoons (1 stick) butter
1 big Spanish onion, chopped fairly fine
1¾ cups arborio rice
1 cup dry white wine (optional)
Three to four 10½-ounce cans low-sodium chicken broth
3 tablespoons finely chopped parsley
⅓ cup grated Parmesan cheese
2 tablespoons heavy cream
Freshly ground black pepper

You can cook the sausages, chicken, and mushrooms first, or you can cook all these things at once as you're starting up the risotto—anyway, it all has to get cooked and, since we have to start somewhere, I'll start with the sausage.

Cook the sausages, either by sautéing them in a tiny bit of olive oil (so they won't stick), pricking each several times with a fork so as to release the fat, or by microwaving between several sheets of paper toweling until they're cooked through. (This takes 15 minutes in my microwave.) When they're cool, slice into bite-size pieces and set aside.

Cook the chicken just till it's done, either by sautéing it in a tiny bit of olive oil or by microwaving in a microwave-safe dish covered in plastic wrap. (About 10 minutes in my microwave.) Don't worry about seasoning it; just get it cooked. When it's cool, chop into bite-size pieces and set aside with the sausages.

In a bowl, cover the dried mushrooms with ½ to ¾ cup water, making sure they're all covered thoroughly but still pretty closely packed. Pat the fresh mushrooms clean with dampened paper towels, cut off the very ends of the stems, and slice, not too thin; an average mushroom could be cut into three or four slices. Melt 1 tablespoon of the butter over medium heat in a fry pan of some kind, then add the fresh mushrooms, stirring frequently as you sizzle them on all sides. When they're browned, add the dried mushrooms and their liquid, which should itself have turned brown by now. At a light boil, keep cooking until all the liquid has disappeared and the mushrooms, both dried and fresh, are a deep musky brown. (The stronger-flavored dried mushrooms will have made the ordinary fresh ones taste like fancy imported ones.) Set aside with the chicken and sausages.

In a big pot (big enough to cook pasta, say), melt the rest of the butter and sauté the onion over lowish heat until wilted but not browned. Stir in the rice, keep the heat low, and heat until the stark whiteness begins to look opaque. Add the wine—or, if you're skipping this, add the first can of chicken broth all at once. Stir to incorporate, and keep stirring every few minutes until the broth evaporates. (If you're working ahead, you can add the wine, stir well, and turn off the burner for an hour or two before continuing.)

Ladleful by ladleful as the rice absorbs each one, keep adding the broth and stirring every few minutes. Taste after 20 minutes or so, and keep tasting every few minutes thereafter, until the risotto begins to taste al dente—not crunchy but still firm to the tooth. When it reaches this stage, stir in the chicken, sausages, and mushrooms, and add a little more broth to keep the risotto creamy as the chicken, etc., heats up. Then add the parsley, Parmesan, and cream, season with black pepper, stir well, and serve right from the pot.

For the salad

6 handfuls salad greens, any kind

Toss with this dressing

Mix all together in a food processor or blender, taste, and add a little more of whatever you can't taste clearly.

Depending on your taste, up to half a head of garlic, with the cloves peeled
As much olive oil as you need
No more than a capful of balsamic or raspberry vinegar
Couple dashes Tabasco sauce
Salt and freshly ground pepper

Add-a-Course Notes

First course: Bruschetta with Red, Yellow, and Green Peppers, page 175.

Dessert: Cherry Clafouti, page 196.

When we see run-of-the-mill fish fillets at a fish store, the flat ones in various sizes with the bones already out, what exactly are we looking at: Is it fillet of sole? Dover sole? Flounder? Mystery fish? Most likely flounder, because true soles are less readily available, usually labeled with exclamation points, and cost more. But a simple piece of flounder fried quickly in a cast-iron skillet is one of the easiest, lightest, most classic dishes around. Sprinkled with parsley, garnished with a lemon wedge, and served with rice, new potatoes, or any other starch and a green vegetable or salad, it's both a satisfying supper and also the kind of meal that people always claim makes them feel virtuous, although only the cook really has a right to that claim for having cooked it without complaining.

Menu

serves four

Fish Fillets with a Drizzle of Green Sauce Served on a Bed of Watercress

Orzo

Grilled Leeks with Parmesan

Here, the fish has what we call in my house green sauce, because it's green. It's actually an idiot's version of hollandaise, made in a blender or food processor, with wilted watercress chopped up in it. Why the watercress? To me, hollandaise is one of the trickiest sauces around: Even if you do everything exactly right, there is simply, as far as I can tell, no guarantee that you'll get rich, thick hollandaise at the end. Many cookbooks offer recipes for blender-made hollandaise—I've tried all of them that I can find, along with every bottled and packaged hollandaise I've ever come across—and they're okay, as far as they go, but nothing like a real hollandaise and therefore a disappointment, if a real hollandaise is what's on your mind. *But:* If you throw in watercress and call it green sauce instead of hollandaise, you'll have a hollandaise-aura backdrop without the stress. There is no chance that this will curdle, although, as with real hollandaise, it may thicken or it may not. With green sauce, it doesn't matter—thick or thin it tastes good and has extra conversational value because it's green.

Orzo is a tiny little pasta each about the size of a big grain of rice, and readily available in many supermarkets and most gourmet shops; they take well to sauces, including a bit of green sauce. Their only disadvantage is that they're slippery little things, and kind of hard to keep on one's fork. As for leeks, they have a bite—especially with a tiny bit of Parmesan—that contrasts well with the simplicity of the fish and orzo. If you tend to keep away from leeks because of all the dire warnings about cleaning away the grit, it's worth a reminder that those of us who cook are *always* cleaning vegetables. Leeks, otherwise easy to prepare, simply need to be cleaned with a little more vigilance.

For the green sauce (a tiny bit on the fish and a tiny bit on the orzo)

1 bunch watercress, washed,
with stems discarded
4 tablespoons butter,
melted but only just
3 egg yolks
2 tablespoons bottled mayonnaise (low fat is okay)
Juice of half a lemon
Pinch of salt
Pinch of cayenne pepper
A few grindings of fresh pepper

First bring 1 cup water to a boil and pour it over the water-cress, which will wilt it. Then melt the butter, either on the stove or in the microwave. Now put the rest of the ingredients—egg yolks, mayonnaise, lemon juice, salt, peppers, and watercress—into a food processor or blender, blend away until the sauce is green, adding the hot butter in a slow stream until it's all gone. If you're not serving it right away, warm the sauce up just before you do. If it's nice and thick, great. If not, too bad, but it's okay.

For the fish

1 bunch watercress, washed,
with stems left on
4 big flounder fillets or
8 small ones
½ cup milk
¾ cup flour
1 tablespoon paprika
Salt and freshly ground pepper
2 tablespoons vegetable oil,
approximately
2 tablespoons butter,
approximately
8 thin julienne strips red pepper
(fresh or from a jar; optional)

Fan the watercress out on a platter big enough to hold the fish fillets—it's fine if they overlap some. The fish should be cooked as close to serving time as possible, so think of this as a last-minute step. Wash and dry the fillets. Put the milk into one flat-bottomed bowl, and the flour, paprika, a sprinkling of salt, and a few generous grindings of pepper, mixed together well, into another flat-bottomed bowl. Bring the butter and vegetable oil to a medium-high sizzle in a cast-iron or other heavy skillet. Dip each fillet first into the milk, then into the flour mixture, then shake off and drop into the skillet. Don't crowd the pan. Fry quickly, turning once only, just a minute or two on each side, and remove to the serving platter, placing the fillets gently over the watercress. Drizzle half the (carefully warmed-up) green sauce over the fillets in a stream—the aim is to show just a hint of green, not obliterate the fish entirely. (The other half gets tossed with the orzo.) If you have the pepper strips handy, lay them in pretty X's over the fillets, and serve.

For the orzo

Follow the package directions and, once the orzo is cooked and drained, toss with the remaining (carefully warmed-up) green sauce.

For the leeks

Cut the root end off the leeks, then cut most of the green end off as well; mostly we want just the white part. Now cut each white part lengthwise into halves, then quarters. So that the julienne strips stay more or less in place, hold each quarter carefully under running water, flipping it a little (as if it were a deck of cards) to get out any bits of grit between the layers. If you want to prepare this ahead of time, you can do all but the Parmesan stage (see below) in advance.

4 big leeks
¾ cup chicken stock, fresh or canned, or ¾ cup lightly salted water
6 to 8 tablespoons grated Parmesan cheese

If you have a microwave, place the quartered leeks cut sides up in a microwave- safe casserole with a flat bottom, trying to keep them as much as possible in a single layer and aiming for an attractive pattern. Pour the stock over them, cover with plastic wrap, and microwave for about 4 minutes before testing for doneness. To test, lift a corner of the plastic wrap, pierce a leek with a knife, and, if the knife slides through easily, remove. If not, keep zapping and testing until it does. When it does, remove the plastic wrap and drain out and discard the liquid, trying to keep your prettily arranged leeks from falling into the sink. (You can hold them in place with a kitchen towel over the plastic wrap, drain out of the exposed testing corner, then remove the wrap.)

If you don't have a microwave, proceed as above in a big fry pan with a lid. Boil gently for about 10 minutes before testing for doneness. When the knife pierces easily, drain away the liquid as best you can, rearranging any leeks that misbehave.

Parmesan stage: Sprinkle the Parmesan over the still prettily arranged leeks in a light but relatively even layer. Put under the broiler just until the Parmesan bubbles and begins to get brown. Serve right away.

Add-a-Course Notes

First course: Caesar Salad, page 185.

Dessert: Basmati Rice Pudding, page 197.

$\mathcal{B}$ack when I was too shy to ask the waiters in Italian restaurants to translate the menu for me, I'd always order veal piccata, because I knew what it was: lemony veal, with capers on top, and parsley.

It was usually too lemony for my taste, but that didn't stop me—at least I knew what I'd get when I ordered it. Later, when I started playing around with the dish at home, I switched from veal to chicken, and didn't pound the cutlets flat, into scaloppine, because I wanted the sauce a little more complex. Scaloppine have to be gotten in and out of the skillet fast, but cutlets are thicker, giving you a little more time to play around. One tablespoon of cream, I discovered, whisked into the sauce at the end, cuts the lemony taste of the sauce (or glaze, really, because there's just enough to coat the cutlets) just enough; the tang's there still, but it doesn't make you wince.

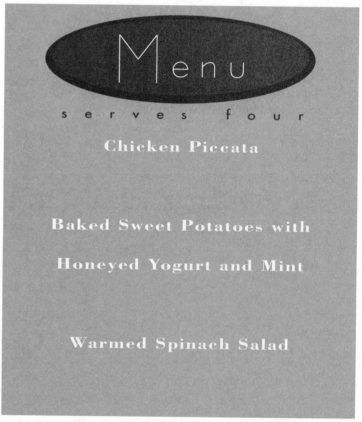

Menu

s e r v e s   f o u r

Chicken Piccata

Baked Sweet Potatoes with

Honeyed Yogurt and Mint

Warmed Spinach Salad

Sweet potatoes are baked just like regular potatoes, and they're wonderfully fragrant when they come out of the oven. Adding honey to the yogurt sweetens it just a little—a nod, perhaps, to the ubiquitous marshmallows that top sweet potatoes every Thanksgiving throughout America. Warmed spinach salad, a variation on a Cobb salad, is a fine way to present spinach, because even people who don't like it much will eat it because nearly everyone likes bacon.

Here, the salad should be served with the rest of the meal, as a vegetable.

For the chicken

Sauté the shallot in the butter and vegetable oil over medium-high heat until wilted. (The shallots may blacken as you cook the chicken, but that's okay.) Now dredge the cutlets on both sides in the flour, put them into the skillet, sauté till they're golden brown on one side, then turn them over. Once you've turned them over, pour in the wine and the juice of a lemon, which will result in a satisfying, momentary whoosh of a sizzle. The wine and lemon will soon boil down to a nice glaze as the chicken finishes cooking. When it's cooked, whisk in the heavy cream until it's incorporated into the sauce. Turn the cutlets once again to coat with sauce on both sides, remove to a platter, sprinkle with salt, grind on some pepper, sprinkle with capers and parsley, and spoon any remaining sauce from the pan over the top. Garnish with the extra lemon somehow.

1 big shallot, peeled and minced
2 tablespoons vegetable oil
2 tablespoons butter
4 plump chicken cutlets
1/4 cup flour
1/3 cup dry white wine
Juice of 1 lemon
1 tablespoon heavy cream
Salt and freshly ground pepper to taste
3 tablespoons capers, drained and chopped
3 tablespoons finely chopped parsley
A second lemon, for garnish

For the baked sweet potatoes

Preheat the oven to 375°F. Wash the sweet potatoes and puncture in several places with a fork, as you would with potatoes to be baked. Bake for up to an hour, depending on their size; they're done when easily pierced with a knife. Meanwhile, whisk together the yogurt and honey. When the sweet potatoes are done, slash them open on top, fluff the pulp a bit, spoon one-quarter of the yogurt mixture on each, and sprinkle each with a quarter of the mint.

4 sweet potatoes, skins left intact
8 tablespoons yogurt
4 tablespoons honey
2 tablespoons finely chopped fresh mint (or parsley, if mint isn't readily available)

For the salad

1 red onion, chopped
3 tablespoons olive oil
1 tablespoon
balsamic vinegar
1 pound spinach, cleaned
and dried
Salt and freshly ground
pepper to taste
2 hard-boiled eggs,
finely chopped
4 slices bacon, cooked and
crumbled into bits
3 plum tomatoes,
finely chopped
2 tablespoons crumbled
blue cheese (optional)

Sauté the red onion in the oil and vinegar until slightly wilted, then add the spinach, tossing in the hot oil only until it's dressed and beginning to wilt. Remove to a platter and season to taste with salt and pepper. Sprinkle the eggs, bacon, tomatoes, and, if desired, blue cheese over the top, and serve while it's still warm.

Add-a-Course Notes

First course: Linguine with Rosemary-Gorgonzola Sauce, page 169.

Dessert: Pear Crisp, page 195.

Swiss chard is one of the great under-used vegetables of our time—cheap, easy, and readily available, at least all summer long. Comparable to spinach, it actually has more presence and texture when it's cooked, and it's never sandy the way spinach is, so it's much easier to clean. It also comes in colors: red-veined or white-veined, and they're pretty mixed together. One confusing thing (to me, anyway) is the stem question: Do you cook and eat the stems, or ribs, as they're sometimes called? The answer is yes, you can, but they take longer to cook, so if you're going to use them, cut and start cooking the stems first. Me, I just cut the stems *off* up to where the leaves begin and discard them wantonly. Swiss chard takes the same amount of time to sauté as scallions do, which is lucky since it goes well with scallions.

This mustard sauce, which has a lot of body, is totally easy to make, and works just as well on chicken, veal, or turkey scaloppine, and also on vegetables. The tarragon isn't essential, either, but I like to leave the sprigs whole and pile them up on top—like a tarragon jungle gym—which makes a grander presentation than little bits of the leaves chopped up. You could use parsley, thyme, or cilantro instead, if that's what you happen to have around.

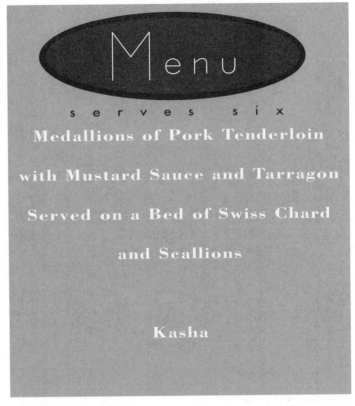

Menu

serves six

Medallions of Pork Tenderloin with Mustard Sauce and Tarragon Served on a Bed of Swiss Chard and Scallions

Kasha

If you don't know it, kasha is a prepared grain that is as easy to cook as couscous, except that it has more bite and a nuttier taste. The taste of couscous would be lost here, because everything else in the meal is so vigorous. Kasha is sturdier, and holds up admirably.

For the mustard sauce

1 shallot
1 teaspoon butter
½ cup dry white wine
One 10½-ounce can low-sodium chicken broth, preferably Campbell's
2 tablespoons dry mustard
1 cup sour cream (nonfat sour cream is fine)
Freshly ground pepper

Chop the shallot coarsely and sauté it in the butter until it's brown around the edges. Add the wine and the broth, and bring to a boil; continue boiling for about 10 to 15 minutes, until the broth is reduced to about ¾ cup, give or take. Strain it, and throw away the shallot. Whisk in the mustard and sour cream until they're blended, and grind in the pepper to taste. (It probably won't need salt at all.) If it happens to be ready early, you can reheat it gently.

For the pork medallions

6 pork medallions
2 shallots, chopped
Olive oil
Few drops of balsamic vinegar
Freshly ground pepper

Have the butcher cut six slices off a loin of pork and pound them flat, or do it yourself, with the flat end of a meat pounder between layers of wax paper.

In a big fry pan, sauté the shallots until they're wilted in enough olive oil to cover the bottom of the pan, then add the medallions, as many as will fit without crowding the pan; you may have to do it in two batches. Sauté over medium heat for about 3 minutes. Just before turning the medallions over, put a few drops of balsamic vinegar into the pan, pouring directly onto the oil, not onto the medallions. (The vinegar will give the medallions a nice glazed look.) Swirl the oil around the pan to distribute it. Flip the medallions, and cut into the center of one after 3 more minutes to see if they're just cooked all the way through. When they are, sprinkle some pepper over them.

They should be lightly browned on the outside, and glazed.

For the Swiss chard

Rinse the Swiss chard and shake off as much water as you can into the sink or out the back door. Cut off the stems to where the leaves begin, and discard. Chop the chard coarsely. Slice the scallions on the diagonal. Melt the oil and butter in a pot with a lid, and cook the chard and scallions over lowish heat, flipping the greens from time to time (an easy way is with two big spoons), and covering them in between. They're done when they're all wilted—you'll be able to tell. Add salt and pepper and serve.

2 bunches Swiss chard, each as big as a nosegay
1 bunch scallions
1 tablespoon vegetable oil
1 tablespoon butter
Salt and freshly ground pepper

For the kasha

Follow the directions on the box.

To assemble: Take the Swiss chard out of the pot, pressing out any residual liquid first by using a slotted spoon. Spoon it onto a platter. Layer the pork on top in a pretty way, spoon on the mustard sauce, and pile on the tarragon sprigs. Serve the kasha on the side.

1 13-ounce box kasha

Add-a-Course Notes

First course: Caesar Salad, page 185.

Dessert: Apple Tart, page 189.

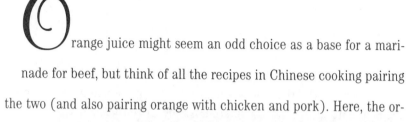

Orange juice might seem an odd choice as a base for a marinade for beef, but think of all the recipes in Chinese cooking pairing the two (and also pairing orange with chicken and pork). Here, the orange juice combines with the hot chili sesame oil (available in gourmet shops and, increasingly, in good supermarkets) as a background flavor but very distinct even so, like a trail of fine perfume left behind after a beautiful woman leaves the room. (Which is not to suggest wearing hot chili sesame oil on your pulse points.) The steak, the Portobello mushrooms, and the dressing all have this faint hot-orange aura, but the rest of the vegetables don't, so it's never overwhelming in a one-dish supper. Because it is a one-dish supper, it's nice to serve the bread really hot, the steak and vegetables warm, and the lettuce room temperature, to vary the temperatures as well as the textures. Not essential, though. If the steak and vegetables cool down to room temp, that's okay, too.

Menu

s e r v e s   f o u r

Composed Steak Salad Marinated in Orange Juice and Hot Chili Sesame Oil

Toasted Garlic Bread

For the marinade and salad

For the salad dressing: Put 2 tablespoons of the orange juice in a bowl big enough to hold the peppers and a vinaigrette. Add ½ cup vegetable oil, 2 tablespoons red wine vinegar, 2 or 3 dashes hot chili sesame oil, salt and pepper to taste, then whisk and correct the seasonings. Put the peppers into the vinaigrette and leave them there.

For the marinade: Take half the remaining orange juice, add to it (this recipe is not very precise because it doesn't have to be) 2 tablespoons vegetable oil, 1 tablespoon red wine vinegar, a couple dashes hot chili sesame oil, and salt and pepper to taste. Add the meat. A good way to marinate the meat is in a tightly closed plastic bag, turning often. The meat should marinate for half an hour to an hour, no longer.

Now using the rest of the orange juice, make the same marinade as above, and brush the mushrooms with it, re-brushing as often as you can for about half an hour.

Bring a pot of salted water to a boil, drop in the potatoes, and cook them for 15 minutes or so, until a knife pierces them easily. Drain and cut them in half, so they'll be able to react to the dressing. Keep them slightly warm, if you can. (If not, don't worry about it.)

Broil or grill the mushrooms first (a grill is great for this), then the scallions. Cut the scallions in half after they're grilled. Keep these vegetables slightly warm, if you can, or don't, if you can't. Now grill the steak to the desired degree of doneness, let it rest a few minutes, then slice on the diagonal.

To compose the salad, put the greens onto a big platter first, then add the potatoes and toss well with the dressing and peppers, whisking the dressing first to make sure it's still well incorporated. Now put the scallions on, in a crisscross pattern, then lay the mushrooms on top.

Make a well in the center of the platter, then layer the steak prettily. Snip the cilantro on top, if you're using it, and serve right away, passing the hot bread.

---

1 cup (freshly squeezed) orange juice

¾ cup vegetable oil

4 tablespoons red wine vinegar

Several dashes of hot chili sesame oil

Salt and freshly ground pepper to taste

1½ to 2 pounds strip sirloin, New York steak, or flank steak

8 Portobello mushrooms, stems removed

16 small new potatoes, washed

1 bunch scallions, green and white parts both, root end cut off

4 big handfuls mixed greens, any kind

1 red pepper, cut into julienne strips

Cilantro (optional)

For the garlic bread

1 baguette
2 tablespoons olive oil
2 cloves garlic, peeled and
cut in half

Slice the baguette in half lengthwise, and toast lightly (probably under a broiler) but don't let it brown. Remove from the oven. Brush the exposed sides lightly with the oil, then rub with the cut side of the garlic and put the bread back under the broiler to let it get lightly golden brown. Serve hot.

Add-a-Course Notes

First course: Pizza (a light one, without cheese), page 179.

Dessert: Suzanne's Honeyed Cheese, page 188.

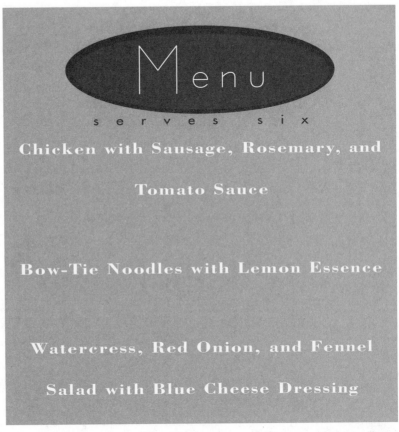

This is a slightly rougher-hewn version of a chicken dish I once had at Orso, a lively bistro in New York. The tomato sauce is fragrant with rosemary, pungent with olives, and creamy, but the waiter told me that the creaminess comes from whisking Parmesan and butter into the tomatoes; there's no cream used at all. I doubt they use canned tomatoes at Orso, but I do and just add a few fresh ones at the end as well, to complicate the texture. The dish is made in three steps—cook the chicken pieces, cook the sausage, make the sauce—then it's all mixed together, peasant style. If there are leftovers, remove the chicken from the bone, and toss the whole thing (chicken, sausage, sauce) into a pasta a couple of nights later. There's no trick here, except to use whole chickens cut into small serving pieces. Don't try, in other words, using whole breasts; it'll taste all right but look really clunky. At the supermarket, you can usually find small fryers all cut up, or else a butcher can do it for you.

I try to refrain from using pasta as a side dish, so that I don't get into the habit of doing it every night, it's so easy and good. However, here the lemony taste is pleasingly sweet with the deeper taste of the chicken. And watercress salad is really light.

Menu

serves six

Chicken with Sausage, Rosemary, and Tomato Sauce

Bow-Tie Noodles with Lemon Essence

Watercress, Red Onion, and Fennel Salad with Blue Cheese Dressing

For the chicken

1 cup dry white wine
Two 3-pound fryers, cut into
serving pieces, or the
equivalent of 5 to 6 pounds
miscellaneous serving
pieces of chicken
1 lemon, halved
1 bunch fresh rosemary
6 to 8 spicy sausages
Olive oil
4 cloves garlic,
peeled and left whole
One 35-ounce can whole,
peeled tomatoes, chopped
and well drained
2 plum tomatoes,
coarsely chopped
3 to 4 tablespoons grated
Parmesan cheese
3 to 4 tablespoons butter
Freshly ground black pepper
1 cup Moroccan (or any
kind of black) olives, pitted

Preheat the oven to 350°F. Pour ½ cup of the wine into a baking pan big enough to hold the chicken (or two smaller ones) and lay the chicken pieces on top, skin side up. Squeeze the lemon halves over the chicken pieces, a few drops of juice on each, then tuck the empty lemon halves somewhere into the pan as well. Snip rosemary (leaves only, no stems) generously over the chicken, so that each piece has at least a little. Leave a teaspoon or two of leaves intact, to put into the sauce. Bake for 50 minutes to 1 hour; they're done when you insert a paring knife into the flesh somewhere and the juice runs clear, not pink. When they're done, turn off the oven and leave them in there to stay warm.

Now cook the sausages, either by sautéing them in the tiniest bit of olive oil, pricking often to release the fat, or by cooking in the microwave between several layers of paper toweling, pricking each in a couple of places first. (In my microwave, this would take about 15 minutes, but the times vary.) When they're cooked through, cut into small pieces.

Now make the sauce. In a big fry pan, sauté the garlic cloves in enough olive oil to cover the bottom until they're lightly browned, then discard. Add the remaining ½ cup wine, the remaining teaspoon or two of rosemary, and the can of tomatoes, stirring at a light bubble until the wine is pretty much evaporated and you're left with a tomato mush. Reduce the heat to medium-lowish and stir in the fresh tomatoes. If you're not ready to serve the meal yet, stop here, turn off the heat, and start again at this point just before you're ready to eat.

When the fresh tomatoes have wilted into the canned ones a little, add 3 tablespoons Parmesan, stir energetically, then add 3 tablespoons butter, and keep stirring until the sauce looks creamy. (If necessary, add another tablespoon butter and/or Parmesan—but it *will* get creamy.) Now stir in the sausages and heat until they're warmed through if they aren't already, then grind in some black pepper and stir in the olives at the last minute.

Put the chicken on a big platter, discarding the remaining pan juices, and pour the sauce over it. Try to serve hot.

For the noodles

Follow the directions on the box.

1 pound bow-tie pasta (or pasta of your choice)

For light lemon sauce, if you have lemon oil

Heat all these ingredients together and toss with the pasta.

2 tablespoons vegetable oil

2 tablespoons butter

½ to 1 teaspoon lemon oil or to taste

2 tablespoons finely chopped parsley, give or take

Salt and freshly ground pepper to taste

For light lemon sauce, if you can't find or don't have lemon oil

Bring the lemon juice, vodka, and oil to a boil, and boil lightly for about 30 seconds, to allow the alcohol in the vodka to evaporate. Reduce the heat to warm, and stir in the butter, lemon rind, heavy cream, and parsley. Add salt and pepper to taste, and toss in the pasta.

Juice of 2 lemons and grated rind of 1

2 tablespoons vodka

2 tablespoons vegetable oil

2 tablespoons butter

2 tablespoons heavy cream

2 tablespoons finely chopped parsley, give or take

Salt and freshly ground pepper to taste

For the salad

2 bunches watercress, cleaned
3 endives, sliced lengthwise into thin julienne, to mirror the length of the watercress
1 red onion, finely chopped

Arrange the endive and watercress prettily on a plate, and sprinkle with the chopped red onion. Drizzle the vinaigrette over the top.

For the vinaigrette

½ cup vegetable oil
⅓ cup finely crumbled blue cheese (Roquefort or Gorgonzola, but the supermarket brands just labeled "blue cheese" are the cheapest)
3 tablespoons red or white wine vinegar
½ teaspoon dry mustard
½ teaspoon paprika
Dash of cayenne pepper
1 tablespoon heavy cream
Freshly ground pepper to taste

The easiest way to mix is to put all the ingredients into a jar with a lid and shake well. Otherwise, whisk well and drizzle lightly over the salad greens.

Add-a-Course Notes

First course: Seasonal Remoulade, page 182.

Dessert: Sweetened Ricotta and Mixed Fruit, page 191.

Old-fashioned French restaurants used to douse all kinds of fish in lobster sauces, and I can still remember how those sauces, infused with sherry, used to taste to me as a kid: dusty. I still don't like them. This lobster sauce is infused instead with the taste of ginger and just a trace of white wine.

Despite the fact that it seems, at first glance, that there are a lot of ingredients in it, it's easy, and it sets off the sweet scallops really well. The bright green arugula wilts a little from the hot pink sauce poured on it, and the red peppers scattered over the top make the dish a triumph of presentation without a lot of trouble.

As for spaghetti squash, it's the great fun food for grownups. It bakes pretty much by itself. Then you cut it in half and, scooping with a fork (forks *do* scoop, in this case), take out the pulp, which looks exactly

Menu

s e r v e s   f o u r

Bay Scallops with Gingered Lobster Sauce Served with Julienned Red Peppers on a Bed of Arugula

Spaghetti Squash with Garlic Sauce

like spaghetti, and tastes fine, too. There is no trick to this, hard to believe as that may sound. It's you, the fork, and the squash, and it will come out in spaghettilike strands. Spaghetti squash takes well to any simple sauce you might put on spaghetti—or simply to butter, a touch of cream, parsley, salt, and pepper. This garlic sauce is also good on a side dish of spaghetti (or a simple piece of fish). It's made with garlic paste, which comes in a tube and keeps in the refrigerator, and in which the garlic is already processed and smoothed out.

For the scallops, the sauce, the arugula, and the peppers

1 knob ginger, sliced into pieces the size of a quarter, unpeeled
1 shallot, coarsely chopped
1 tablespoon vegetable oil
1 tablespoon butter
Juice of half a lemon
One 10½-ounce can chicken broth
½ cup dry white wine
1 lobster tail, fresh or frozen
1 teaspoon tomato paste
1 tablespoon hot chili sesame oil
Pinch of ground ginger
2 tablespoons heavy cream
Freshly ground black pepper to taste
2 red peppers, cut into thin julienne
1 quart bay scallops, fresh or frozen
1 pound arugula, washed and dried well
4 tablespoons coarsely chopped cilantro

In a big skillet or pot, sauté the ginger slices and the chopped shallot in the vegetable oil and butter until golden. Add the lemon juice, chicken broth, white wine, and bring to a boil. Reduce to a gentle boil and add the lobster tail, cut into five or six pieces. (Add it now whether it's precooked or not—doesn't matter. You just want to impart the taste of the lobster to the broth and, even if the meat gets tough, you'll be chopping it up anyway. We're trying to draw out the flavor here.) Boil this way, at a comfortable boil, for about 15 minutes, until the mixture begins to turn a golden brown. Now pluck out the ginger, and let the mixture cool a little before processing. (Or cool it down with a couple of ice cubes.) Add the tomato paste, the hot chili sesame oil, a pinch of ground ginger, to reinforce the ginger taste, and the heavy cream. Put into a blender or food processor and blend or pulse until the lobster is all chopped up and the sauce is smooth. Season with black pepper to taste.

Put the sauce back in the skillet and add the peppers, keeping the heat at medium-low until the peppers begin to wilt, 3 or 4 minutes. Now add the scallops, stirring frequently until they turn from pink to white, which will take just a few minutes.

When the scallops are ready, heap the arugula onto a big platter and spoon the scallops, sauce, and peppers evenly over the top. Sprinkle the chopped cilantro over everything, and serve.

For the spaghetti squash

Preheat the oven to 350°F. Although it might be fun to see a spaghetti squash explode, if you'd rather it didn't, pierce it with a sharp knife all the way to the center three or four times; this enables the steam to escape. Bake it whole in the oven for 30 to 45 minutes, or even a little longer. When it pierces easily with a knife—as opposed to how hard it was to pierce before cooking—it's done. Cut in half lengthwise, wearing oven mitts. It will probably already be forming strands. Remove the seeds, then scrape the flesh with a fork, twirling to remove each forkful into a big bowl. Toss with the garlic sauce, and serve hot.

1 spaghetti squash (these come big: try to find one of the smaller ones)

For the garlic sauce

Melt the butter, heat up everything else, whisk to incorporate the garlic paste, and toss with the spaghetti squash.

2 tablespoons butter
2 tablespoons garlic paste from a tube or to taste
2 tablespoons vegetable oil
4 tablespoons finely chopped parsley
Salt and freshly ground pepper to taste

Add-a-Course Notes

First course: Ham Mousse with Melon, page 170.

Dessert: Demitasse Chocolate, page 192.

When a leg of lamb is butterflied, all it means is that the bone has been removed so that it can lie flat—and then it's cooked like a steak, ideally on a gas or charcoal grill or else broiled. This is one cut of meat that does benefit from a (simple) marinade; then, after it's cooked, it's sliced thin, and the slices are presented on plates or a platter in a pretty fan shape. Rosemary and mint are traditional with lamb, and here, there's a trace of rosemary in the marinade, but the sauce is a port wine sauce, not thick or heavy like a gravy, just a thin, flavorful dressing. Often legs of lamb appear butterflied on the shelves of supermarkets (sometimes nice ones are imported from New Zealand, and they're shrink-wrapped); if not, the butcher will do it. Tell him how many you're serving, because legs of lamb come in all sizes.

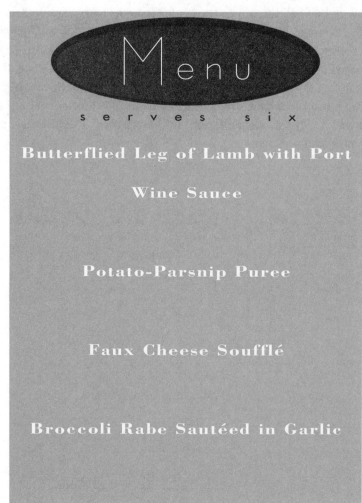

Menu

serves six

Butterflied Leg of Lamb with Port Wine Sauce

Potato-Parsnip Puree

Faux Cheese Soufflé

Broccoli Rabe Sautéed in Garlic

A puree is basically a mashed-potato-type dish that's made with other vegetables—practically any other vegetables, from broccoli to peas to such autumn root vegetables as celeriac, turnips, sweet potatoes, or parsnips. Here, the potatoes serve as a base from which to set off the sweeter parsnips; celeriac or turnips would work as well as the parsnips. Sometimes, too, cooked, peeled apples or pears are pureed and thrown in as well; once you're comfortable with the technique—which is to say after you've made a puree once—you can use whatever's around.

Miraculously, this faux soufflé (no eggs to separate and beat into peaks) puffs up just like a real soufflé although, in my experience, it sometimes deflates between the time you remove it from the oven and the time it reaches the table, even if you don't stop anywhere else first. Thankfully, this does nothing to wreck the taste or your ability to cut it into perfect slices (small slices; this is one of those delicate-little-portion dishes). All it does is make it look more like a pretty Yorkshire pudding than a soufflé, and you might want to think of a different name for it if you're serving it on the flat side: cheese pudding?

As to broccoli rabe, this is a vegetable that, so far as I know, didn't exist when I was a kid but seems to be everywhere now. (Maybe it's replaced wax beans, which were everywhere when I was young but now seem to be extinct.) The flavor is slightly bitter—some people like it and some people don't—but it's a good vegetable here to balance the sweetness of the puree and the richness of the soufflé.

For the lamb

½ cup olive oil
2 tablespoons balsamic vinegar
3 tablespoons fresh rosemary leaves, cut from the stem
1 teaspoon salt
Freshly ground pepper
1 butterflied leg of lamb to serve six (actually, a 4-pounder is about as small as you'll get and is usually enough to serve eight—but leftovers are great in a salad, sandwiches, or with any extra sauce warmed and spooned onto room-temperature lamb)

Mix together the oil, vinegar, rosemary, salt, and pepper, and marinate the lamb with it, either on a platter or in a tightly sealed plastic bag, turning frequently, for at least half an hour, or as long as you want, within reason.

When it comes time to cook the lamb, baste it as you go with any remaining marinade (don't worry about any bits of rosemary sizzling into it; that's okay), start by broiling or grilling 10 minutes per side, then check for doneness. Most people like it done medium-rare to medium.

For the port wine sauce

1 shallot, minced
2 tablespoons butter
One 10½-ounce can chicken or beef broth
¾ cup port wine
Half a lemon, juice squeezed out
6 whole cloves or ¼ teaspoon ground cloves
¼ teaspoon ground mace
Pinch of cayenne pepper
¼ teaspoon balsamic vinegar
Freshly ground pepper
½ to 1 tablespoon Kitchen Bouquet
3 tablespoons minced fresh chives or parsley

Sauté the shallot in the butter until wilted, then add the broth, wine, lemon (squeeze out the juice first and save it for the broccoli rabe), cloves, mace, cayenne, vinegar, and pepper and bring to a boil. Boil away for a while until the mixture reduces significantly; you only need ½ to ¾ cup to pour lightly over the lamb. Once it's reduced, taste it, and stir in half a tablespoon Kitchen Bouquet, taste again, and stir in another ½ tablespoon, if needed. (You'll be able to tell.) Stir in the herbs. Serve hot, drizzled over the lamb.

For the puree

Cut the potatoes into quarters and boil them in lightly salted water until they pierce easily with a fork, but before they begin to turn grainy, probably no more than 15 minutes. In another pan of lightly salted boiling water, cook the parsnips until they, too, pierce easily with a fork, about 10 minutes. Now put the potatoes through a ricer or food mill, which will do away with the potato peels, or mash well any other way except in a food processor, which will turn them to glue. The parsnips, though, can be processed to a pulp in a food processor. Energetically mix together the mashed potatoes and the parsnips, add butter and heavy cream (start with $\frac{1}{3}$ cup, then increase as necessary), salt, pepper, and a little nutmeg to taste. Serve hot.

3 big potatoes

Salt

5 parsnips, peeled and cut into 1-inch chunks

2 tablespoons butter

$\frac{1}{3}$ to $\frac{1}{2}$ cup heavy cream

Freshly ground pepper to taste

Freshly grated nutmeg to taste (a little goes a long way)

For the faux soufflé

Preheat the oven to 450°F. Try to imagine all these ingredients in a casserole or soufflé dish, and pick one they won't fill more than two thirds full, to enable the soufflé to rise. Do not grease the dish. Beat the eggs and cream until foamy (an egg beater helps, and it only takes a couple of minutes), add the rest of the ingredients, stir well to mix, and bake for 25 minutes. Try to open the oven door as little as possible during this time. Cut into slices or wedges and serve hot.

2 eggs

$\frac{2}{3}$ cup heavy cream

$\frac{3}{4}$ cup grated Monterey Jack, Swiss, mozzarella, or cheddar cheese, or a mix (low fat is okay)

$\frac{3}{4}$ cup grated Parmesan cheese

Dash of Tabasco sauce

Pinch of cayenne pepper

Pinch of salt

Freshly ground pepper

For the broccoli rabe

2 to 3 stalks broccoli rabe
per person
3 cloves garlic, peeled
3 tablespoons olive oil
Juice of 1 lemon
Salt and freshly ground
pepper to taste

Wash the stalks, pulling off any extra leaves as you would with broccoli. Sauté the garlic in the oil until browned, then discard. Over medium heat, sauté the broccoli rabe until it's al dente, sprinkle with the lemon juice, season with salt and pepper, and serve.

Add-a-Course Notes

First course: Linguine with Rosemary-Gorgonzola Sauce, page 169.

Dessert: Mix-and-Match Strawberry Sauce, page 193.

Part Four

ADD-A-
COURSE
NOTES

To me, the offering of a first course (or appetizer, or starter; it's all the same idea)—a tiny-portioned delicacy to whet the appetite before the entree—is the signal that a meal is to be special. In restaurants, when I can get away with it, I'll order a salad and a couple of first courses and call it a meal: There's an *elegance* to first courses that makes one notice and savor the tastes more than usual. A first course also suggests participation in a ceremony, not just a Pavlovian response to a dinner cue. An offering on a small, pretty plate, whisked away to make room for the entree—never enough, I like to think, to do much damage to even the strictest diet, or at least worth the indulgence.

Apart from the suggestions offered here, there are many other ways to come up with ideas for first courses. Small just-a-taste servings of an out-of-the-ordinary salad served on a bed of lettuce or watercress. (Another bonus: Many first courses can be summoned to do double duty as lunch.) A cup of soup, like squash soup or a variation thereof (page 207), served hot or cold, depending on the season and your preference. A bit of fresh or leftover risotto or any kind of pasta, portions half of what they would be when served as a main course. In high tomato season, sliced tomatoes and fresh basil with a drizzle of olive oil and balsamic vinegar, salt and plenty of pepper, and any of the following: red onion slices, fresh or smoked mozzarella, black onions, goat or feta cheese, avocado.

Or you can just pull out part of the main course and set it off as a starter—asparagus, cauliflower, or broccoli with a sauce, a pretty collection of seasonal grilled vegetables (peppers, summer squash and zucchini, eggplant, onions) served with black olives, capers, and a drizzle of olive oil. Or new potatoes, topped with sour cream and supermarket-bought caviar or salmon roe.

In a classic soup-to-nuts sense, a formal meal should include something fishy, something meaty, vegetables certainly, possibly a soup or a salad with a touch of fruit and cheese, something sweet. The first course is where you can fill in whichever of these is missing from the courses that will follow it. And start the ceremony.

Linguine with Rosemary-Gorgonzola Sauce
For six starter portions

This starter course is practically foolproof, fragrant with rosemary and pungent with Gorgonzola. That it tastes so rich (tastes downright fattening!) is deceptive; the ratio of cheese to broth is much lower than you'd think. Even so, it's too intense to serve as a main course, but perfect in starter portions, particularly preceding lamb, pork, veal, or duck. I use the cheapest domestic Gorgonzola I can find, but the rosemary has to be fresh. I've tried the recipe with dried rosemary, and it doesn't work nearly as well; fresh rosemary releases its oils into the broth, which makes all the difference. Other than that, it doesn't matter if the sauce turns out a little thicker or thinner, so long as all the elements are in it.

The sauce could also be used on veal chops or scaloppine, or on pounded chicken breasts.

2 shallots
2 tablespoons olive oil
One 10½-ounce can chicken broth
½ cup dry white wine
2 to 3 tablespoons fresh rosemary leaves, chopped fine
Freshly ground pepper
An average pie-piece-size wedge Gorgonzola
Salt
1 tablespoon heavy cream, approximately
1 pound linguine

Chop the shallots fine, and sauté them in the olive oil until they're wilted but not browned. Dump in the chicken broth and the wine, and bring to a boil. Snip in as many rosemary leaves as you can manage now, so that they'll boil along with the broth to release their fragrant oil. (Try not to put any of the stems in.) While you're at it, you can also grind in the pepper, about 1 tablespoon of it, at this time. Keep boiling until the broth is reduced by about half. If you're serving it right away, you could put the salted pasta water on now; if you're making it ahead, it can sit around for a few hours right on the stove without anything horrible happening.

Turn down the heat and add the Gorgonzola; you can crumble it or just drop in the whole thing, doesn't matter. Simmer until it melts into the broth. Now add the cream and whisk the mixture with a wire whisk so as to incorporate everything. When you're ready to serve it, whisk again, toss it with the pasta, and that's about it.

Ham Mousse with Melon
(or Figs or Peaches)
To serve six

*1 pound baked ham from the deli; no
need to have it sliced*
3 tablespoons mayonnaise (low fat is fine)
1 tablespoon softened butter
1 teaspoon mustard, preferably Dijon
2 tablespoons dry port wine
*½ teaspoon cayenne pepper or
more to taste*
Freshly ground pepper

This is a variation of the slice-of-prosciutto-draped over-a-slice-of-melon theme. The mousse gets better if it sits in the refrigerator for a while, so you might want to make it earlier rather than at the last minute.

It's good as a starter when a light fish course is to be the entree, or if you want to introduce a bit of meat into a predominantly vegetarian meal. If you had to make an hors d'oeuvre—if you were giving a cocktail party, say—you could also serve this mousse with crackers.

For the mousse

Cut the ham into chunks, removing any rind or fat, put it into a food processor, and pulse until it's the texture of hamburger. Stir in everything else and, if possible, chill for at least a couple of hours before serving. Bring it back to room temperature again before serving, so that the butter isn't hardened.

For the fruit

*1 ripe melon—honeydew, cranshaw,
muskmelon, or cantaloupe (or a dozen
figs or 6 ripe peaches)*
Juice of 1 lemon
1 tablespoon orange juice
Dousing of dry port wine (optional)
Freshly ground pepper

Cut the melon into bite-size pieces (or quarter the figs or slice the peaches), and toss with the lemon and orange juices, and the dousing of port if you like. Grind on some black pepper and toss again. Chill the fruit until you're ready to serve it. (By the way, if your big ripe melon turns out to be grainy and not so great, you can do some damage control by also sprinkling in a pinch of ground cloves, which will add another sutble flavor and help detract from the melon itself.)

Each person gets a small scoop of the mousse on his or her plate; the cut-up marinated fruit goes around it.

Seafood Salad
To serve six

This is a simple salad but an elegant one, with the distinct flavors of the squid, shrimp, and scallops tasting amazingly *clean*. As for the beans, I added them once to stretch the salad because extra guests were coming at the last minute, and liked the results so much that now I always add them; they also make the salad cheaper all around. The feeling of this dish is light, because I use vegetable oil instead of olive oil, so that what you taste is the fish, not the dressing. Champagne vinegar makes it seem to sparkle. It's very good served before poultry of any kind, or before a light meat entree.

If you're squeamish about squid, it's a good idea to get over it, since it's surely our most underused treat from the sea. It's cheap, readily available frozen (and already cleaned), and delicious cooked in pasta (with tomatoes, garlic, and black olives); fried (as in fried calamari) in flour or bread crumbs; stuffed (with, for example, pesto, bread crumbs, and plum tomatoes); in seafood stews; and so on. And it's about as nutritious as any food there is. If you're *really* squeamish about squid, however, you can skip the scallops, too, and make a version of this salad with just a triple quantity of shrimp and the same amount of beans and everything else.

⅓ cup vegetable oil, plus some for the pan
Old Bay or another seafood seasoning
18 large shrimp
8 medium squid, cleaned and cut into thin rings
1 pint bay scallops
Champagne vinegar (or white wine vinegar)
1 lemon
Salt and freshly ground pepper
1½ cups (about ¾ can) small white beans, rinsed and drained
4 tablespoons finely chopped fresh mint

Cover the bottom of a medium fry pan with vegetable oil, sprinkle about 1 teaspoon seafood seasoning into it, and sauté the shrimp over medium heat until they're just cooked through. Remove them, and put them into a strainer to drain off any excess oil.

Now sauté the squid in the same oil, stirring often. (It's important to do the shrimp before the squid, because the squid give off a liquid in which you can lightly poach the scallops.) The size of the squid rings, the level of heat, and the kind of pan you're using will vary the cooking time, but it will probably be about 3 minutes. They'll firm up right away, turn whiter, and begin to release their liquid. Try to take them out just at the moment you begin to notice the first signs of their edges curling—they're definitely done then; you don't want the edges to curl any more. If you have one, use a slotted spoon to remove the squid from the pan into the strainer with the shrimp so as not to lose the liquid; if not, just do your best.

Put the scallops into the squid liquid, with the heat very low, stirring them around until they turn white on all sides, about 2 minutes. Drain them, too, with the squid and shrimp.

When the seafood has cooled, cut the shrimp into thirds so that they're about the same size as the scallops.

Pour ⅓ cup vegetable oil into a measuring cup. Now squeeze in the juice of a lemon, then fill with champagne vinegar to the half-cup mark. Put the mixture into a bowl, add a sprinkling of salt and freshly ground pepper, and whisk until the ingredients are blended. Taste the dressing; you should be able to taste all three ingredients at the same time. If not, add a touch of whichever ingredient doesn't come through clearly.

Put the seafood into a bowl and toss well with the dressing. Stir the beans in carefully, so they don't get all squashed. Stir in the chopped mint just as you're about to serve the salad; stirring it in too soon will make the mint soggy. I've served it with various garnishes—mixed lettuce underneath, a few black olives on the side, a few big capers on top—but I then decided it speaks perfectly well for itself, and now I serve it unadorned.

Christopher's Smoked Fish Salad
To serve six

This salad is the inspiration of my friend Christopher Idone, writer, culinary genius, and excellent houseguest; he often does the cooking when he visits. I gave him a hard time the first time he offered to make this salad, the ingredients for which sounded thoroughly weird to me: smoked fish and *grapefruit?* It was absolutely delicious, surprising, easy, and it looks beautiful on a platter. It's a good starter for lighter entrees—veal or chicken entrees, or pasta served as a main course.

The salad greens are the key here: You need heavy greens, like escarole, romaine, or curly endive, to carry the rest of the ingredients; a lighter, more delicate lettuce, such as Bibb, Boston, or leaf lettuce, would collapse and flatten under the weight of the fish and grapefruit. (It's hard to remember the names of all these greens, but they're labeled in the supermarket.) Heavier greens, in other words, balance the dish better.

It's not always a good idea to chop onions and peppers in a food processor, since this method slashes them up in such a way that a lot of their juice drains out; if you chop them by hand, very little juice is lost. For this dish, though, it's easiest to chop the onion and pepper in a food processor, then put the bits—along with the juice—into the vinaigrette to soak.

This salad is a composed salad, which basically means that the ingredients are put together in a specific order. A warmed baguette is nice to have on the table with it.

²/₃ cup olive oil

4 tablespoons balsamic vinegar

1 teaspoon dry mustard

Salt and freshly ground pepper

1 red pepper

1 red onion

1 big pink grapefruit, or two small ones

½ cup walnuts, coarsely chopped

1 pound filleted smoked bluefish, whitefish, or any other fleshy salt- or fresh-water fish (except smoked salmon)

1 big head escarole, curly endive, or romaine lettuce, or two smaller heads, washed and coarsely chopped

1 bunch cilantro

First make the vinaigrette, whisking together the olive oil, balsamic vinegar, mustard, a couple of pinches of salt (not much salt, though, since smoked fish tastes salty), and a generous amount of pepper.

Pulse the red pepper and onion in the food processor until they're finely minced, then stir them up with the vinaigrette and set aside.

Peel and section the grapefruit, and slice each section into two or three pieces, removing as much of the pithy white stuff as you can. There's a trick to doing this. Cut each end off the grapefruit with a paring knife, then cut off the peel and outer membrane to expose the fruit, feeling your way carefully so as to avoid wasting any actual grapefruit. Pick any grapefruit section, cut inside the membrane carefully, and open it up. You can pull the grapefruit section right out, leaving the membrane intact. Now keep pulling out the sections all the way around the grapefruit—the membrane will, in the end, be in one piece, and the sections will be about as perfect as they can get. Or just do the best you can in your usual way.

To chop the walnuts, put them between sheets of wax paper and hammer at them a while with a hammer or meat pounder until they're about the size of the peanut pieces in crunchy peanut butter.

To compose the salad, put the greens on the platter first. Whisk the vinaigrette, pepper, and onion mixture again, pour it over the greens, and toss well. Now put the grapefruit sections on top, and with your hands fluff up the greens around them; you want the vinaigrette to touch the grapefruit, but you don't want the grapefruit to sink to the bottom of the greens.

With your hands, separate the flesh of the fish from the skin, pull it apart into bite-size pieces (*small* bite-size pieces), and place the pieces all over the top of the salad, fluffing up the greens again around the fish. Sprinkle on the walnuts, snip cilantro generously over the whole thing, and serve.

Bruschetta with Red, Yellow, and Green Peppers

(or any combination thereof)

To serve six

Learning to roast peppers is like learning to ride a bike: After it clicks, you know how to do it forever. With roasting peppers, it will click the first time and, from then on, you'll have at your disposal one of the great appetizers of all time. Peppers of any color work fine, but it's prettiest if you have a mix: All green will taste okay, but won't have much plate appeal. Red and yellow mixed are very pretty—orange, too, are sometimes available—but green peppers are sometimes cheaper, so I usually throw in a couple of those as well. (Even brown peppers, when mixed with red, yellow, and green, look nice.) Allow one pepper per person, plus one extra, the way you put in an extra spoonful of coffee for the pot.

Serving peppers as bruschetta—that is, on bread that's been toasted and brushed with olive oil and garlic—rounds out the dish and gives it some crunch.

For the peppers

Wash the peppers and make sure they're thoroughly dried. Put them under a broiler (or on a gas grill, which is easier), and blacken them on all sides and on the bottom as best you can; you'll see the skin blister and separate from the flesh. When they're pretty well blackened, put them into a brown paper bag, close it tightly, and let them steam in their own heat until they're cool enough to handle.

7 peppers of mixed colors
3 cloves garlic, peeled
1 tablespoon olive oil
Salt

When you open the bag, you'll see seven peppers as deflated as yesterday's balloons. Handling them gingerly, peel off the skin (this will be easy to do), remove the seeds, cut away the core, and cut them into evenly sized strips about an inch wide. They'll be juicy, having released their oil de pepper or whatever it's called; try to save as much of this oil (which is delicious) as possible, by keeping a bowl or platter nearby to catch it while you're cutting up the peppers.

When all the peppers are cut up, cut the garlic cloves in half, then toss them among the peppers, add the olive oil and a sprinkling of salt, and refrigerate for a while, if you have time, to allow the garlic to release its own essence into the peppers. Before serving, bring the peppers back to room temperature and remove the garlic.

For the bruschetta

1 big baguette
3 cloves garlic, peeled
2 tablespoons olive oil

Slice the bread into twelve not-too-thin rounds; they should be about an inch thick. Toast them until they *feel* toasted but aren't yet browned. Brush one side of each piece of toast with olive oil, cut the garlic cloves in half, then rub the cut sides of the garlic over them. Toast the oiled sides of the bread for less then a minute, until the oil sizzles and the exposed side browns a bit, then serve two pieces of each per person with the peppers spooned on top.

Smoked Salmon with Dilled Honey-Mustard Sauce

To serve six

Quite possibly the most welcome appetizer there is, smoked salmon is one of the great first courses of all time. Even without doing a single thing to it except piling it onto a platter, you get full style and taste credit; all by itself it makes a meal feel elegant. However, smoked salmon is still something that you've *bought*, not made, so by doing a little something extra to it, you get extra credit. This sauce, which is also delicious with sausages or drizzled onto plain grilled fish or chicken, is creamy and piquant at the same time. You can serve it all by itself, or with the optional extras noted below. Toast points give it body and crunch, so they're nice to include, but the salmon and the sauce alone can carry the course. Honey mustard, which is mustard sweetened with honey, is readily available in jars at most supermarkets. If you don't happen to have any, you can also mix honey with Dijon mustard, for *almost* the same effect.

For the salmon

12 to 18 slices smoked salmon, depending on their size
6 slices thin-sliced white bread, crusts removed, toasted, and each
    slice cut into two triangles; or thin-sliced black bread or baguettes
    (optional)
6 tablespoons drained, finely chopped capers (optional)
6 tablespoons finely chopped red onion (optional)
6 tablespoons finely chopped hard-boiled egg (optional)

For the dilled honey-mustard sauce

2 tablespoons honey
mustard (or 1 tablespoon
each Dijon mustard
and honey)
4 tablespoons olive oil
2 tablespoons heavy cream
or half-and-half
2 tablespoons finely
chopped dill
Freshly ground pepper to
taste

With a wire whisk, whisk all the ingredients until they are very well blended and creamy. (It will seem gloppy at first, but soon smooth right out.)

To assemble: Toast, if desired, goes on the bottom, with the slices of smoked salmon laid out flat on top. A little of the sauce gets trickled over the top. The optional condiments can be passed in small bowls or sprinkled around the edges of each plate as a garnish.

Pizza
To serve six

Delicate slivers of thin-crusted appetizer pizza are about as much like paper-plate-defying slices of pizza-parlor pizza as foie gras is like liverwurst—same family, perhaps, but a relative many times removed. These portions are fragrant with herbs and light, whetting your appetite for the entree, not filling you up for the next three days. They're not piled high with all-you-can-eat ingredients, but treated lightly, with sparse but seductive snips of herbs and various cheeses, vegetables, fish and meats, in practically infinite combinations. Best of all, you don't even have to make the dough for the crust.

Most supermarkets sell balls of prepared pizza dough, which looks exactly like—and *is*—dough perfectly adequate for making excellent pizza. At my favorite supermarket, it comes in a little plastic see-through box, although I've also seen it in plastic bags or pouches. It has yeast in it and so will rise all by itself. It's therefore best to buy it within a day or two of when you plan to use it for optimum freshness, but it can also hang around until the expiration date on the package.

At a yard sale once, I bought a wonderful round pizza pan, a huge one like those used in pizza parlors, and I'm happy to have it even though it's too big to fit in my oven. You don't need a pizza pan; a cookie sheet works fine. You also don't need to be able to flip the pizza up toward the ceiling with your hands, although it's very tempting. Rolling out the dough with a rolling pin (or wine bottle, or whatever you can find) as thin as you can on a lightly floured surface will do the trick nicely; you want the sensation of crispy thin pastry, not thick dough. Then put the dough onto a cookie sheet (or shape it into smaller, individual-size pizzas), flute the edges with your fingers, and put on a topping. Among the mix-and-match toppings that work really well:

- A very light brushing of store-bought marinara or tomato sauce. The average 12-ounce jar is more than enough for one ball of pizza dough;
- Brush a tiny bit of olive oil, sprinkle with crumbled cheese like goat cheese (it doesn't even have to cover every inch of the pizza) and pitted black olives, then snip rosemary leaves or sprinkle thyme leaves on top, and grind on fresh pepper;
- Anchovies or sardines, if you like them, go with whatever you like them with;
- For meats, try pizza-parlor meats of choice: sausages, pepperoni, prosciutto;
- Or try ricotta cheese (drain it in a strainer for a while first), particularly good when you add chopped fresh spinach and a minimal grating of fresh nutmeg;
- Fresh or smoked mozzarella, grated, or grated Monterey Jack, with fresh thyme and a few scattered chopped or sliced plum tomatoes (drained for a little while first)—light or low-fat cheeses work really well;
- Mushrooms of any kind, thinly sliced and pre-sautéed in the tiniest bit of olive oil, go particularly

well with a light brush of tomato sauce and mozzarella, Monterey Jack, or Gorgonzola;

- A thin brushing of (store-bought) pesto is also a good base. Try adding crumbled goat cheese, black olives, a few chopped sun-dried tomatoes, toasted pine nuts, plus a few snips of fresh basil;
- You can omit cheese entirely, by rubbing lightly with olive oil, then add a drizzle of pesto, and a few tomatoes and black olives;
- Julienned peppers, lightly sautéed, of all colors, broccoli or leeks cooked al dente, plum tomatoes, drained—all kinds of vegetables can be scattered (in a *thin* layer) over pizza with a light base of tomato sauce and cheese;
- Pay attention to pizza parlor menus for more ideas.

A sample pizza recipe

1 Spanish onion, peeled, halved, and sliced thin
12 plain old supermarket mushrooms, approximately, wiped clean, bottoms of stems sliced off, and mushrooms sliced thin
1 ball pizza dough
One 12-ounce container or jar marinara or tomato sauce
One 8-ounce package shredded mozzarella cheese (low fat is okay)
Freshly ground black pepper

Preheat the oven to 400°F. In a skillet, sauté the onion and mushrooms until they're lightly browned in as little olive oil as possible, about 1 tablespoon. (The mushrooms will release their juice to help the cooking process.) Remove from the heat.

On a lightly floured surface, roll the dough over and over patiently; it will begin to get quite thin. Let it get as thin as you can, while still being able to handle it. Either cut it into individual-size pizzas (each about as big as a saucer) or shape it into one big one. (The shape doesn't have to be absolutely perfect; Michael once very proudly made one, as someone pointed out, more or less in the shape of the United States—but it's not hard to get it fairly symmetrical.) Put the dough onto an ungreased cookie sheet and pinch or flute the edges slightly, rolling over a bit as necessary to hold the sauces.

With a brush or small spoon, brush a light coat of the marinara or tomato sauce over the pizza; with a 12-ounce container of it, you should have a little left over to do something creative with. Now, with a slotted spoon to get rid of any remaining olive oil or juice, spread the mushroom-onion mix over the pizza as evenly as you can. Sprinkle the shredded cheese over that, grind a little black pepper over the pizza, then put in the preheated oven. In 20 to 25 minutes, the crust will have turned brown, and the pizza will be sizzling. It's ready. Remove from the oven, wait a couple of minutes for the sizzling to die down, cut with a sharp knife (unless they're individual pizzas, in which case serve them as is) into appetizer-size portions, and serve.

Sizzled, Flavored Meat on Shredded Lettuce

To serve six

This light first course features meat, and goes well with a vegetarian (or close to vegetarian) entree, or a light fish dinner. The meat—chicken, lamb, or pork—is sizzled until slightly browned, to give it some crunch; the shredded lettuce gives it more. The vegetables give it color and texture, the hot chili sesame oil and orange juice give it surprising flavor, and, all in all, it's pretty easy. By now, ground chicken is a staple at most supermarkets, and you can often find ground lamb and pork as well. If not, the butcher will grind it for you.

In a big skillet, sauté the onion, red and green pepper, and garlic in the vegetable oil until wilted, then remove with a slotted spoon. Now sauté the meat over fairly high heat in the same skillet, and keep poking at it with a wooden spoon as you do; you want to get it well browned, almost crispy. When it is, put the vegetables back in, stir the mixture together, then add the orange juice, wine, and several dashes of hot chili sesame oil. As you're letting the liquids boil away (fairly gently boil), shred the lettuce, julienne the scallions, and mix together with another dash or two of the hot chili sesame oil. Make a bed of the lettuce-scallion mixture on each of six appetizer plates. Add the salt and pepper, taste the meat mixture, correct the seasonings, and then spoon it evenly on top of the lettuce-scallion beds, and garnish, if you like, with a few snips of cilantro and a curl of pickled ginger.

3 tablespoons chopped onion, approximately

3 tablespoons chopped red pepper (from a jar is okay), approximately

3 tablespoons chopped green pepper

4 cloves garlic, finely minced

3 tablespoons vegetable oil

1 pound (or a little more) ground chicken, lamb, or pork

Juice of 2 oranges

½ cup dry white wine

Several dashes hot chili sesame oil to taste

1 small head iceberg lettuce, shredded as if you were using it to make coleslaw (a mandoline is a great help)

1 bunch scallions, green and white parts both, chopped into julienne strips

Salt and freshly ground pepper to taste

Cilantro and sliced pickled ginger from a jar as garnish (optional)

Seasonal Remoulade
To serve six

Celery root (also known as celeriac and unrelated to celery itself)—like such other root vegetables as turnips and parsnips—is at its peak in the autumn, and one of the culinary ways to mark the season's passing is to serve julienned strips of cooked celery root, cut like the potato sticks you buy in a can, tossed in a remoulade, a sauce both sweet and pungent, in the autumn. If you've never cooked one before, a celery root is a knobby and unpromising item to behold, looking more as if it should be thrown away than cooked, much less eaten. But give it a chance. When you cut away the dirt-covered, knobby outside, the flesh inside is pure white; when cooked until tender, chopped into julienne strips, tossed in this (easy) sauce, and served at room temperature or very slightly chilled, your first course will feel like a grand harvest.

Celery root season is short, but remoulade season can be stretched out by changing the vegetable. Fresh beets, either the deep purple or the yellow ones, turn up in the market off and on throughout the year. Baked (as you would a potato), quartered or sixthed, sections spread out like flowers, one per person, the beets are brought to room temperature or served slightly warmed and topped with the remoulade sauce. In the same way, cooked artichokes can be served with remoulade sauce on the side. One sauce: Three starters.

For the celery root

Salt
6 celery roots, each the size of a big grapefruit, or 4 to 5, if they're much bigger— about three pounds total
1 lemon

Bring a pot of salted water, big enough to hold the celery roots, to a boil. Gingerly, so as not to waste the flesh, cut away and discard the knobby outsides of the roots, to expose the white flesh inside. Don't worry if a few brown spots remain; these can be removed easily after cooking. Cut the roots into quarters and sprinkle with lemon juice to ward off discoloration. Don't worry, either, if the roots begin to discolor a little, anyway; the sauce will even out the color. Drop the pieces of celery root into boiling water, and cook until a paring knife pierces them easily. Cooking time will vary according to the size of the pieces, how old the celery roots are to begin with, etc., so begin checking after about 12 minutes. They should take somewhere between 15 and 20 minutes. When the knife pierces them easily, remove from the boiling water, run cold water over them well to stop further cooking, and cut into evenly sized julienne strips, removing any brown bits that remain. Spoon the sauce (below) over, mixing as you spoon, to incorporate it into the julienne strips: You want them barely covered, not drowning in sauce.

For beets

Preheat the oven to 350°F. Wash the beets well, prick several times with a fork so as to let the steam escape, and bake as you would a potato, for 35 to 45 minutes, depending on their size (huge ones might take a little longer). They're done when a knife pierces them easily. Remove from the oven, and let them cool until they're comfortable to the touch. Section them into quarters or sixths, either peeling them or leaving the skin in place—your call, but I think it's more earthy and rustic to leave it in place; also it's less likely that the sections will break. (The skin isn't edible, however, so you have to tell people to eat only the flesh.) Arrange the sections as if they were petals, and trail the sauce (below) over the sections lightly, so that each bite will yield a trace of sauce.

6 fresh beets, as close as possible to the same size, purple or yellow, skins left on

For artichokes

Bring a big pot of salted water to a boil, big enough to allow the artichokes to tumble around a bit, so they're not too crowded. Cut off the stem, so that the artichoke will be able to stand up straight, as it were. Now pluck off browned or sharp leaves at the bottom of the artichoke and, with a sharp knife, cut the top inch or so off altogether. With a scissors, go around the artichoke, cutting off the sharp points of any particularly prickly leaves. (I wonder who first figured out that these odd things are edible?) Cut the lemons in half, drizzle the lemon juice over the artichokes, then toss them in the boiling water. Depending on their size, it may take 20 to 40 minutes for them to cook. They're ready when you scoop out one with a strainer and the bottom leaves come off easily, and when the remains of the stem are easily pierced with a paring knife. Serve hot or room temperature.

Salt
6 artichokes, as close as possible to the same size
2 lemons

For the remoulade sauce

½ cup mayonnaise
(low fat is fine)
2 tablespoons sour cream
(no fat is fine)
2 teaspoons Dijon mustard
or more to taste
Dash Tabasco sauce
Dash Worcestershire sauce
1 tablespoon capers,
drained and finely chopped
2 tablespoons chopped
fresh herbs (chives, parsley,
tarragon, or a mixture)
Freshly ground pepper to
taste

Mix all together, taste for seasonings, and serve over the vegetables as described above.

Caesar Salad
To serve six

It's odd, how often I see people ordering Caesar salad in restaurants and, at the same time, how seldom people make it at home, when it's so easy. Why? Possibly because the ceremony of composing the salad with grand flourishes at the table seems a little theatrical. (If so, you can do it in private, in the kitchen.) Maybe, too, it's that raw eggs make many of us nervous; in that case, the eggs may be coddled, or dropped into boiling water for a minute, no longer than a minute and a half. Finally, it could be because the world is divided into two kinds of people: those who like anchovies and those who don't. I happen not to (unless they're freshly caught anchovies, which we rarely get in this country), but I compromise with a little bit of anchovy paste (no bones!) from a tube, which tastes fine to me, and anchovy lovers don't complain, either. Rather than making croutons, it's easier to take a baguette, cut it in half lengthwise and make garlic bread. The bread goes on top of the salad after it's dressed in a big *X* and people just tear off a chunk as they serve themselves. (It doesn't get soggy this way, either.) The only other trick is to gather all the ingredients before you start. Rushing around isn't going to help the salad one bit.

Put the garlic cloves to soak in the oil for as little as half an hour or as long as a day. Stir the oil a few times if you're only soaking the garlic for a little while. Toast the bread lightly under the broiler, removing it before it browns. Brush lightly with a bit of the olive oil, rub with the cut end of the garlic, then put back under the broiler to brown. (The bread needn't be hot when you serve it.) Now arrange the lettuce leaves in a bowl or on a platter, ripping the larger ones to the size of the smallest. Just before you're ready to serve, break the eggs over the lettuce, then toss well with your hands. Remove the garlic cloves from the oil and discard. Now stir the anchovy paste, mustards, lemon juice, Tabasco, Worcestershire, and salt into the oil, whisk until blended, and pour over the salad. Pour the Parmesan over, too, and toss well again, using your hands. Grind black pepper generously on top, taste, correct seasonings as necessary, put the bread in an *X* on top, and serve.

4 cloves garlic, peeled and cut in half

½ cup olive oil

1 big baguette

2 to 4 heads romaine, depending on size, coarse outer leaves removed, the rest washed and dried well

2 eggs, raw or coddled (boiled for 60 to 90 seconds)

1 teaspoon anchovy paste

½ teaspoon dry mustard

½ teaspoon prepared mustard, like Dijon

1 lemon

Dash of Tabasco sauce

Dash of Worcestershire sauce

Dash of salt

½ cup freshly grated Parmesan cheese

Freshly ground black pepper to taste

Ten Desserts

$\mathcal{I}$t is said that people who cook well don't, as a rule, like to bake, which is why good restaurants generally have a chef chef and also a pastry chef. I myself say it a lot: I hate to bake. I think it's because there's an air of whimsy and experimentation to cooking; one gets seized with the inspiration of adding a little peanut butter or cayenne pepper or banana puree to a dish, and sometimes it works out okay. This is *creative*, in a way, and gives the process an element of surprise, whether it works out or not. When it comes to baking, on the other hand, you had better follow the measurements and directions to the letter; there's very little room for cutting corners. It's a rigid just-stick-to-the-facts pursuit—improvise and you'll be sorry.

Which is why bakeries come in so handy, and guests who offer to bring dessert. And weeknights, when nobody really expects much and grocery-store sweets seem indulgent enough. Weekends, however, call for dessert. While it's true that most people are on diets all the time and claim they don't eat dessert, it's also true that the *reason* people are on diets all the time is that they *do* want to eat dessert. Guests expect it: Sending guests off without dessert would be like going to work without your shoes. Which is not to say that dessert need be a grand or elaborate presentation, just something to close the ceremony. So every cook should have a few desserts in his or her repertoire. (Not too many.)

How do you decide what to serve for dessert? I always start by thinking: "Was there fruit somewhere in the dinner?" If not, then fruit in some variation for dessert. "Was there cheese—and I don't mean just a sprinkling of Parmesan—featured in the meal?" If not, cheese for dessert. (Or fruit and cheese—both very easy to work with, even if you have to omit fruit or cheese from somewhere else in the meal.) "Was there something cream-based?" If not, then something creamy is okay for dessert. Very light meals call for a heavier dessert, and vice versa. Ice cream or chocolate go with just about anything. If someone gives me a box of chocolates, for instance, it goes right into the freezer and comes out again when I need a quick dessert: pears, a wedge of any kind of veiny cheese (Gorgonzola, Saga, Stilton), and a plate of chocolates.

Can you do store-bought? Sure. Just take away the paper doilies and don't try to pass it off as your own, because that will always backfire.

All these recipes, by the way, specify six servings—and they will indeed serve six. They'll also serve eight (or sometimes ten, if someone declines) if you make the servings smaller.

Suzanne's Blueberry (Cake Mix) Cobbler
To serve eight to ten

2 pints blueberries, rinsed
1 box Jiffy yellow cake mix (first choice) or Duncan Hines yellow cake mix (second choice)
8 tablespoons (1 stick) butter, melted
Ice cream, crème fraîche, or heavy cream to serve alongside

My friend Suzanne doesn't remember where she got this recipe, but it has the feel of one that's been passed around forever. Make it once, and you'll never need the recipe again, it's that easy. All told, this will serve six to ten people, twelve if you make the portions pretty small. If I were serving fewer than six people, I might halve the recipe; more likely, I'd just heat the leftovers up the next day. It should be served with ice cream, crème fraîche, or a bit of heavy cream.

Preheat the oven to 350°F. Dump the blueberries into a casserole or baking dish big enough to hold them plus a box of cake mix. Put dry cake mix over the blueberries, covering them as evenly as possible. (Do not *make* the cake mix, just pour it dry.) Drizzle melted butter over the top. Bake for about 45 minutes, or until nicely browned and crispy on the top. You could also run it under the broiler for a few minutes at the end to brown. Serve hot (reheat it if you've made it earlier), with ice cream, crème fraîche, or heavy cream.

Suzanne's Honeyed Cheese

Not the same Suzanne as above, but another friend, who happens to be in the writing-about-food business herself, a wonderful cook, and who offers here her recipe for the Best Dessert/Most Elegant Dessert. In her words:

"I had this first at Tre Vesale, the inn in Umbria owned by the winemakers, the Lungarotti family. Here goes: a small piece of really wonderful fresh local goat cheese, covered with rich, local honey and served with Vin Santo, the lovely Italian dessert wine. Since then, I've had variations of this all over Italy—including, last week in Rome, Gorgonzola and red clover honey. It is a divine dessert—the essence of sweet, rich satisfaction. Can serve with biscotti but not necessary. The only reason it's not served here must be because it's too easy. There are no rules, except to use creamy cheese and heavenly honey. And it's a great chance to serve dessert wine—which so rarely goes with dessert."

She's right. Allow 3 or 4 tablespoons of really good cheese per person, and honey to taste.

Apple Tart

To serve eight

A tarte Tatin is a French apple tart with the crust on the bottom and the apples (arranged prettily) in a kind of glaze on the top. Very elegant. It gets made upside down, most easily in a cast-iron skillet, with the apples going in first, on the bottom, and the pastry tucked around it on top. When it's baked, there's one major moment of courage required: Shortly after it's removed from the oven, you have to put a platter on top of the skillet and flip the whole very hot tart onto it in one reason-defying motion. It's worth practicing this with a hot, empty skillet a few times before you actually try the tart. It can be done, though, and once you do it, you will have made a very impressive dessert.

Frozen puff pastry obviously makes such a tart much easier to make, and Pepperidge Farm makes a particularly good one. Once you've got apple down pat, you'll also know how to make tarts of pear, peach, and apricot.

A tart in a 12-inch skillet will serve eight, and you can adjust the portions down a bit if you want to use a smaller skillet.

Preheat the oven to 375°F.

Peel and core the apples, and slice into fairly thin wedges. First scrape the lemon of its zest (yellow part only, and chop fine), then sprinkle the zest and drizzle the lemon juice over the apples. Now melt the butter in a 12-inch skillet over medium-lowish heat, add the sugar and stir fairly steadily as it begins to caramelize. You want it to turn the color of mahogany. Once it does, after 10 or 12 minutes, remove from the heat and spread the glaze evenly across the bottom of the pan with a wooden spoon. Drop the apple slices into the glaze (they'll sizzle in a satisfying way) in a pretty pattern, beginning on the outside and working your way in. When you've covered the bottom of the skillet with apple slices, you'll still see some glaze showing through—fill these holes with apples, too, but try to keep the whole thing pretty close to one layer of apples. The tart, when flipped, has to be fairly flat.

6 to 8 apples suitable for baking, like Granny Smith or McIntosh (not Delicious)
Juice of 1 lemon, plus 1 teaspoon or more of its zest
8 tablespoons (1 stick) butter
¼ cup sugar
1 sheet frozen puff pastry, thawed and rolled according to package directions
1 egg
¼ cup milk

Now take the rolled-out pastry sheet and spread it over the bottom of the pan, tucking in the edges around the apples. (If it breaks, just patch it up as best you can, but all the apples have to be covered.) Whisk together the egg and milk, and brush (with a clean paintbrush or pastry brush) over the pastry.

It should take about half an hour for the tart to cook—the crust will become golden brown all over. (Check it after about 25 minutes.)

Use heavy pot holders or oven mitts to take it out of the oven and, after waiting 5 minutes to let it set, invert it onto the platter. It needn't be served hot, but it should definitely be served proudly.

Sweetened Ricotta and Mixed Fruit
To serve six

Sweetened ricotta is delicious, not fattening at all, and thoroughly easy to make. You serve a couple of tablespoons of it as if it were ice cream, with the fruit around it. The recipe is easily halved or doubled. Two tips: The first is that expensive vanilla extract from the gourmet store is much, much better than supermarket brands. And the second is that fresh whole nutmegs are so much better than ground nutmeg that it isn't even funny. Whole nutmegs come in jars in the spice section, you grate them (on the smallest edge of your regular grater, or you can get a nutmeg grater), and they stay fresh practically forever. You can also grate nutmeg onto squashes, into purees, in creamed spinach, over creamed soups—a little goes a long way. So use whole nutmeg, or else use cinnamon.

For the fruit, you can use peaches, any kind of berries, fresh apricots, grapes, nectarines, melons.

One 15-ounce container ricotta cheese (low fat is fine)

2 teaspoons vanilla extract

Juice of half a lime, plus 1 teaspoon, give or take, of grated lime peel (it's easier if you grate the peel before cutting the lime)

2 tablespoons sugar

½ teaspoon freshly grated nutmeg or a little more to taste

For the ricotta

Mix it all up in the food processor, and that's it.

For the fruit

Mix all the ingredients together except the mint, which if you're using it should go in at the last minute. Refrigerate for a couple of hours if you have time, stirring occasionally, to let the juices blend.

3 to 4 cups mixed fruit

½ cup orange juice

2 tablespoons brown sugar

¼ teaspoon balsamic vinegar

2 tablespoons any fruit-flavored liqueur (optional)

2 tablespoons chopped fresh mint (optional)

Demitasse Chocolate

To serve six

1 cup semisweet
chocolate chips
1 cup light cream, scalded
(heated, that is, to just below
the boiling point)
2 egg yolks
3 tablespoons brandy (or
rum, Scotch, or any fruit-flavored liqueur) or
1½ teaspoons vanilla
1 tablespoon grated orange
rind (optional)
Finely chopped
hazelnuts (optional)
Strawberries as garnish
(optional)

One New Year's Eve when I had a dozen people coming to dinner and was desperate for an easy but elegant dessert, I came across this basic recipe in Peg Bracken's *I Hate to Cook Book*; she calls it pot-de-chocolate. Peg (she's the kind of writer you feel you can call by her first name) had come across it in a blender booklet. I also found it in another book, *Darling, You Shouldn't Have Gone to So Much Trouble*—so I think it's pretty fair game. I've added the hazelnuts, and serve strawberries (frozen are okay, but defrost them first; fresh ones with stems are prettier) as a garnish. I've also added grated orange rind, which I found in a more difficult recipe for pots de crème. The reason I changed the name is that it helps me to remember how to serve it—in demitasse cups or small glass goblets. It's rich, and a little goes a long way.

Put everything in the blender or food processor except the strawberries and hazelnuts. As Peg puts it, ". . . Blend it till the racket stops." Pour it into a big bowl or directly into little cups or glasses, and refrigerate for at least 3 hours. Serve with the hazelnuts sprinkled on top and strawberries on the side, or just serve it.

Mix-and-Match Strawberry Sauce
For eight "puddles"

This is not a recipe that lifts taste to an exalted new dimension, but it has essence of strawberries, which just about everybody likes, it's light, it's pretty, and it's dessert. You can serve it with ice cream, just about any kind (creamy pistachio, vanilla fudge, any of the chocolates); it looks nicest if you make a puddle of sauce under the ice cream rather than pouring it on top. You can add chopped salted nuts, or not. A puddle of it is also nice under puddings, tapiocas, and garden-variety custards. A puddle of it over or under store-bought chocolate cake or pound cake gives a homemade touch to a fairly ordinary dessert. Just pour it out from a decorative pitcher. The ingredients are practically the same as for the mixed fruit, page 191. This is because brown sugar works better than white with fruit; it gives it a glazier quality. The orange juice provides a base into which the fruits can release their liquid. As for the tiny bit of balsamic vinegar, it's classic with strawberries, and I've just carried that over to other fruit compote-type fruits as well. If you want to make extra, by the way, this sauce keeps for a long time in a tightly covered jar.

Half a 20-ounce bag frozen strawberries, approximately, thawed

½ cup orange juice

2 tablespoons brown sugar

¼ teaspoon balsamic vinegar

2 tablespoons any fruit-flavored liqueur (optional)

Mix it all up in a blender or food processor till smooth, and serve cold with whatever you're serving it with.

Peter's Chocolate Cake

To serve six

One 8-ounce box semisweet
chocolate baking squares
2 tablespoons flour
2 tablespoons sugar
6 tablespoons butter,
softened
2 eggs, separated
1 to 2 tablespoons confectioners' sugar

This is simply my favorite chocolate cake in the world—very dense, thin, and sophisticated, no frosting but a light sprinkling of confectioner's sugar over the top. It's the kind of cake you imagine sitting on a pastry cart at a really good French restaurant. My friend Peter made it for dinner the very first time I met him, and I had to track him down relentlessly all the way to a fax machine in California to make him give it to me. It requires that you have a 6-inch springform pan, which is the sort of thing that makes people who hate to bake leery. All it means is a pan with a removable bottom, which comes out when you release the latch on the side. It's worth it to have this transcendent cake in your repertoire.

Preheat the oven to 450°F. Prepare the 6-inch springform pan by cutting a sheet of wax paper to fit the bottom, and buttering it on both sides. (Do one side, then put the buttered side down, and butter the second side.) Following the instructions on the box, melt the chocolate squares either on the stovetop or in a microwave oven. Stir in the flour, sugar, and butter, making sure the sugar gets dissolved. Let the mixture cool slightly for a minute or two, then stir in the egg yolks. Now beat the egg whites, preferably with an egg beater, until they're frothy with little bubbles, and mix them into the batter well, but not more than necessary. Pour the batter into the pan, and bake for 15 minutes. Cool completely in the pan, then remove to a pretty plate. Sprinkle the confectioner's sugar through a strainer so that it goes on as a fine powder.

Pear Crisp

To serve six

This is a slight variation on apple crisp, but you could certainly use peeled apples (or peeled peaches) in place of the pears. To peel fresh peaches, drop them into boiling water for a minute or two, and the skins will come off easily. Sometimes crisps are disappointing in that the crisp-to-fruit ratio weighs heavily in favor of fruit. This isn't the case here.

Preheat the oven to 350°F. Toss the pears together with the lemon juice and liquor, if desired. Add the 2 pinches of each of the spices, toss again, and lay on the bottom of a greased casserole.

In a separate bowl, mix together the flour, nuts, both kinds of sugar, salt, and spices, then, with your hands, knead in the butter until the batter is well blended and crumbly in texture. Spoon or spread the topping evenly over the pears, bake for 35 to 45 minutes, until the crisp is—you guessed it—lightly browned and crispy on top. Serve hot or warm, with heavy cream or vanilla ice cream.

7 pears, peeled, cored, and fairly evenly sliced

Juice of 1 lemon, plus 1 teaspoon of the rind, grated fine

¼ cup Poire Williams, Scotch, or any fruit-flavored liqueur (optional)

2 pinches each ground cloves, mace, and cinnamon, or any combination thereof, for the pears

1¼ cups flour

½ cup finely chopped walnuts or pecans

½ cup sugar

½ cup brown sugar

Pinch of salt

Pinch each of ground cloves, mace, and cinnamon, or any combination thereof, for the topping

8 tablespoons (1 stick) butter, softened

Heavy cream or vanilla ice cream to serve alongside

Cherry Clafouti
To serve six

2 cups pitted cherries, approximately, drained of their juice
3 tablespoons confectioners' sugar
1 teaspoon almond or walnut extract (sold by the vanilla extract at supermarkets and gourmet shops—more expensive extracts make a difference)
1 cup flour
1 cup milk
2 eggs
2 tablespoons sugar
½ teaspoon salt
Ice cream, heavy cream, or crème fraîche to serve alongside

This is another variation on the fruit-and-pastry drill and, although it has a very odd name (the accent's on *fou*), it's probably the simplest of all to make. It looks and tastes like a simple cake replete with cherries. It's better to use canned cherries or those in a jar than fresh, because (a) they're already pitted, and (b) by soaking in the can or jar, they get waterlogged, and the juice releases itself into the pastry in a nice way. Also, you want cherries packed in juice, not in a thick syrup that will just get in the way. Ice cream, heavy cream, or crème frâiche is served on the side. No doubt this could be made with other fruits from a jar or can, but I've never tried it.

Preheat the oven to 400°F, and butter a pie pan or something about the same size. In one bowl, toss the cherries with 2 tablespoons of the confectioners' sugar and the almond or walnut extract. In a second bowl, dump in the flour, milk, eggs, sugar, and salt. This batter is supposed to be smooth, not frothy, so use a spoon to stir it up just till all the lumps are out and the batter is smooth.

Pour half the batter into the pie plate (or whatever), then spoon the cherries on top, then pour on the rest of the batter. (It's okay if some cherries are visible from the top.) Bake for 35 to 45 minutes (check after 30), until it's puffy and lightly browned on top; you can stick a toothpick in and see if it comes out clean to be sure. Remove from the oven, and sprinkle the final tablespoon of confectioners' sugar on top. Serve hot or warm, with the ice cream, heavy cream, or crème fraîche alongside.

Basmati Rice Pudding
To serve eight

Most rice pudding recipes call for leftover cooked rice, but who ever has leftover cooked rice untouched by herbs, nuts, curry powder, or dribblings of sauce? Nobody I know. And who wants to cook rice simply to have it left over in order to make rice pudding? Nobody. The other problem with rice pudding is: What do you serve it with? If with dinner you've served pasta, grains, or rice itself, isn't rice pudding redundant?

This rice pudding, which starts with uncooked rice, is so easy that it can be the centerpiece when you're planning the meal: Start with the rice pudding first, then work backward. You'll find that the meals that seem to match rice pudding are suppery meals in sensibility, not dinnery meals. Rice pudding is cozy winter food, comfort food for all ages, and so what should it come after? A supper of a big bowl of store-bought soup thick with vegetables (no rice), a crisp green salad and a torn-off piece of steaming hot bread. Leftover chili. A vegetarian melange of grilled vegetables served with a poached egg. A simple meal of broiled chicken, sausages, or fish and a salad or green vegetable. So the pudding becomes the starch of the supper, but served sweetened, and as a separate course.

Basmati rice, which is slightly nuttier than plain white rice, imparts a nice bite to the pudding, but plain white rice works just as well. The only other thing to remember is that the pudding has to bake for two hours start to finish, so count backward from the time you want to serve supper.

One way the world is divided, I've noticed, is between those who like raisins in their rice pudding and those who don't. How nice it would be if all our differences were as easily resolved as this one: Raisins are optional.

For the rice pudding

Preheat the oven to 325°F. Butter a casserole big enough to hold the rice once it doubles in volume as it will when it cooks. Mix the eggs together in a small bowl with a little of the milk, then pour everything else into the casserole and stir. Put the casserole into the oven, and stir once after half an hour. It will take almost exactly 2 hours to cook. Check as the time approaches by tasting a little of it with a spoon. Serve it hot, or at least warm.

2 eggs

4 cups milk

1 cup basmati rice (or any kind of white rice)

1 teaspoon good vanilla extract

4 to 5 tablespoons sugar, depending on your sweet tooth

¼ teaspoon salt

½ teaspoon freshly ground nutmeg or to taste (optional)

½ to ¾ cup raisins (optional)

Five Easy Lunches

*L*unch can really intimidate you if you let it.

If you've ever gone to someone's house for lunch, as I have, and been served dinner food—poached salmon with dilled homemade mayonnaise, for example—it can really make your heart sink. If poached salmon in full regalia is *lunch,* then what do you do for an encore? What's dinner?

Cooking elaborate lunches for people is a chore that's best avoided. It's thankless. You won't get dinner-level credit, it cuts into your day too much, and, if you have to cook dinner as well, that's far too much time for anyone to spend in the kitchen over the course of a single day. I'm perfectly happy to *eat* poached salmon, etc., for lunch somewhere else; I just don't want to go to that kind of trouble at home. To avoid it, master the attitude, as I have, that lunch is a casual soup-and-sandwich affair, and stick to your resolve. No matter who's stopping by, keep lunch deliberately carefree, and poach the salmon for dinner. Soup and/or sandwiches or, if you really get into a pinch, serve the fritatta below or one of the selections in the chapter on first courses.

Soup, in particular, can be really easy. There are plenty of good canned soups—minestrone, hearty vegetable soups, creamy tortellinis—in the supermarket; you can even mix two different kinds together (e.g, a minestrone with a pasta fagiole, which is pasta and bean soup). You can give them your own imprint by sprinkling with fresh Parmesan, chopped fresh parsley, basil, or chives, and freshly ground pepper, which give them the texture of fresh. A dollop of yogurt or low-fat sour cream can help chilled summer soups like gazpacho; a dollop of room-temperature goat cheese can give canned vegetable soup a kind of tang. Or you can add to each bowl (or mug or cup—I like serving soup in mismatched teacups) a spoonful of store-bought pesto, chopped fresh plum tomatoes, or leftover vegetables, minced.

If you're feeling unusually reckless, most gourmet shops offer a pot of hot, freshly prepared soup at lunch-time: Why not serve that? If you're feeling unusually *ambitious,* there are a lot of soup kits available commercially, packets with dried beans of various kinds and herbs already built in. Usually you have to chop some onion, carrot, celery, and simmer them for a couple of hours, but they infuse the house with a warming soupy quality. Served with warm fresh bread, a bowl of black olives, a wedge of cheese, a saucisson or some sliced salami (like a sandwich but all spread out—in keeping with the soup-and-sandwich theme), and a tossed salad if you feel like going for broke, lunch actually ends up being elegant, in a homey I-just-tossed-this-all-together way.

When it comes to sandwiches, how can you really go wrong? We all love sandwiches, probably even more than we love poached salmon, if we're honest about it. With all the fresh breads available, and the endless variety of condiments, meats, vegetables, and cheeses to put into it or onto it, certainly a sandwich remains something you can serve with pride, to anyone.

One trick I picked up somewhere (stole from a hotel in Europe, actually), which anyone can accomplish with a gas or propane grill, is *grilling* bread for sandwiches instead of toasting it in a toaster. Most of us have been grilling hot dog and hamburger rolls for years, but other bread tastes better grilled, too: baguettes, big round peasant loaves, even English muffins. Obviously, no sane person would go to the trouble of building a charcoal fire just to toast some bread, but if you already have a gas grill, it's just one more good use to put it to. A basket of grilled bread for breakfast, served with soft Bel Paese cheese the way it was served in that European hotel, is thoroughly grand. Bread grilled at lunchtime is just as good.

Granted, it's not fancy food, but what could be nicer than a BLT at the height of fresh tomato season, in August and September? Extra chicken poached or grilled specifically for sandwiches never goes to waste. Leftover steak of any kind makes great sandwiches, as do leftover pork, turkey, and meat loaf. Leftover lamb makes wonderful hot sandwiches, with the lamb warmed and leftover sauce or gravy drizzled on top. Fancy bread, Brie, and prosciutto are grown-ups' ingredients for grilled ham and cheese, the children's staple. Building one's own sandwich from a variety of cold cuts, mustards, etc., remains, for me, one of life's great pleasures. Even better is eating it.

Better-Than-Usual Tuna Sandwiches
To serve six

Making tuna salad this way changes it from the usual tuna-and-mayo extravaganza into a salad that's tastier, more complex, pretty to look at, even exalted, by tuna salad standards. Children like it, adults like it, you'll like it; the effort-to-praise ratio is quite high with this dish. You could double the recipe or halve it, and it's delicious left over or served with crackers.

You could serve it on any kind of bread toasted or grilled. Usually I just pile it open-faced style on grilled slices of peasant bread, to be eaten with a knife and fork.

1 carrot
1 red onion
2 hard-boiled eggs
One 12¼-ounce can water-packed white-meat tuna, drained
3 tablespoons finely chopped parsley (preferably curly)
Mayonnaise (low fat is okay)
Freshly ground pepper
Bread

One by one, grind up the carrot, onion, eggs, and tuna in the food processor until they're crumbly, about the texture of hamburger. Chop the parsley by hand. Put all the ingredients into a bowl, add just enough mayonnaise to bind the salad, and lots of ground pepper. If you have time, it's a good idea to make this salad a couple of hours ahead of time, so that the flavors will have time to meld in the refrigerator. (Half an hour in the freezer will help, too.) Bring it back to room temperature before piling it onto slices of bread. If you have any left over, by the second day the salad might be a little watery on the bottom of the bowl. This is just the result of the vegetables releasing their water, and doesn't matter a bit. Just stir the salad again before reserving.

Curried Chicken Salad
To serve six

6 boneless, skinless
chicken breasts
1 red onion, finely chopped
(optional)
2 stalks celery, finely
chopped (optional)
2 hard-boiled eggs, mashed
with a fork (optional)
Mayonnaise (low fat is okay)
2 tablespoons chutney
or to taste
3 tablespoons curry powder
or to taste
Freshly ground black pepper
Crumbled walnuts to sprinkle
on top (optional)
Cilantro to sprinkle on top
(optional)
Bread

There's an expensive gourmet takeout shop near where I live that makes great curried chicken salad—at something like thirty dollars a pound. This curried chicken salad is much cheaper, and pretty close. Chutney is the ingredient in the sauce (along with mayonnaise and curry powder) that draws it all together and gives it its resonance, if chicken salad can resonate. One thing: Curry powder loses its zing pretty fast, so even if you end up using it only once a year, it's worthwhile buying a fresh jar of it from time to time.

Some people like little chunks of apple or pineapple in chicken salads, but here the chutney takes care of the fruit department. Most of the other ingredients, however, except for the chicken itself and the sauce, are optional. If you want to serve pineapple with it but not *in* it, fresh or canned sliced pineapple, preferably broiled or grilled, makes a good side dish, particularly with fresh mint snipped over it.

As with the tuna salad above, it's okay to toast or grill the bread and serve it on the side, so that turning it into a sandwich becomes optional. It's also easy to make this recipe for more or fewer people by adding more or fewer of each ingredient.

The easiest way to cook the chicken is to poach it, but you could certainly sauté it gently (in vegetable, not olive, oil) if you wanted. It doesn't have to be cooked elegantly. It just has to get cooked somehow. To poach it, pile the breasts in a pot with a lid, add a dash of chicken Bovril if you have it, 1 tablespoon curry powder, and—if you have them around—a cut-up onion, a carrot chopped coarsely, and a couple of stalks of celery, also chopped coarsely. Add water to cover the chicken breasts. Bring to a boil, reduce to a healthy simmer, and cut into the breasts after about 20 minutes. When they're white all the way through (it might take longer, depending on their size and your simmer), they're done. Dump them out of the pot and let them cool. You can also microwave them, in a microwave-safe dish covered in plastic and sprinkled lightly with curry powder and a couple of drops of water; this might take about 10 minutes.

Cut the chicken into big bite-size pieces, and put them into a bowl. Throw in the onion, celery, and eggs, if you're including them. Add just enough mayonnaise to bind, the chutney, the remaining 2 tablespoons curry powder, and a few grindings of black pepper. Mix well, using your hands if you want to make it easy. Now taste it. Add more curry powder, chutney, and pepper to taste.

Here, too, this dish is better if refrigerated for a couple of hours (or put in the freezer for half an hour) before serving, to allow the flavors to blend. Sprinkle with walnuts and chopped cilantro if you want before serving with bread—warmed, toasted, or grilled.

Lobster (or Shrimp) Rolls
To serve four to six

There are plenty of offerings from the sea that can land in sandwiches, and make lunch an elegant and easy affair, while still keeping the meal casual. (They're not necessarily as cheap as peanut butter and jelly, but sometimes the effect is more important than the cost.) Among these haute sandwiches are smoked salmon on a bagel or baguette, with scallion-studded cream cheese, red onion, capers, lemon juice, and ground black pepper; crabmeat from a can with a little mayonnaise, red onion, and celery, served on a hot-dog roll; and the king of seafood sandwiches, the lobster roll.

Perfect lobster rolls are deceptively simple sandwiches; whatever the season, they evoke summertime and the sea. They're a treat for lunch—fun, not somber. Grown-ups are always as delighted with them as children are, and frozen lobster tails can bring the coast of Maine right into your kitchen anytime. You could also substitute shrimp for the lobster (not canned ones, though—jumbo ones, cut up, are preferable), and make shrimp rolls.

Good cooks are always trying to put their own spin on lobster salad, ruining it every time, in my opinion. Sometimes they use homemade mayonnaise, which lacks the sweetness of commercial and tastes all wrong. Sometimes they bring out the tarragon, which makes lobster salad taste too French. Curry powder is disastrous: The lobster-roll experience is meant to evoke New England, not Bombay. So keep it simple.

A pound of lobster meat will yield four to six lobster rolls, depending on the ratio of lobster to roll. The only absolutely essential ingredients are lobster and mayonnaise (I prefer Hellmann's for this, and the full-strength kind, although the light is okay, too); the rest are for show. To be East-Coast authentic about it, the hot-dog rolls should be the center-split kind, not the side-split kind, although that's negotiable, too. If the lunch is to be an occasion, you could serve coleslaw (page 125) and homemade potato chips (page 129), or you could buy coleslaw and potato chips at the store.

For the lobster salad

1 pound cooked
lobster meat
2 stalks celery, minced
(optional)
Mayonnaise
4 to 6 toasted hot-dog rolls,
preferably center-split
Paprika, for sprinkling lightly
on top (optaional)
A few drained capers
(the fat kind, not the little
ones), to sprinkle atop each
lobster roll (optional)

Cut the lobster meat into chunks (not little minced pieces), add celery if desired, bind with mayonnaise, and stir well. Load it into the toasted hot-dog rolls evenly, sprinkle (a *little* bit, not a lot) paprika on top, if desired, and sprinkle on the capers, too, if desired.

Fritatta
To serve six

A fritatta is neither soup nor a sandwich, but actually an egg pie with stuff in it, a good one at that and certainly easier to make than a perfect omelette. I'm including it here because once in a while, if you have to entertain at lunch, you might want to serve something showier than soup and sandwiches, but without getting into the poached salmon realm. Served with hot bread and a green salad of some kind, it makes a cozy lunch (or supper), one with dozens of variations once you get the hang of it.

Some fritatta recipes are truly alarming, suggesting that you flip the pie out of the pan and onto a platter, then flip it back. This recipe, you'll be happy to learn, is flip-free. You make it in a cast-iron skillet (or a casserole, or any oven-worthy pan), and cut it like a pie. It can be served hot or even at room temperature, if lunch takes longer to get under way than you thought.

The eggs are beaten together and poured over a collection of chopped vegetables, meats, herbs, so that each wedge is full of the tastes and textures of whatever you've decided to add—see below for suggestions. With a sprinkling of Parmesan on top, the fritatta is baked until it sets, then broiled for a couple of minutes to make the cheese all brown and bubbly.

There is no exact recipe, because this fritatta is a catch-as-catch-can dish, preferably using a week's worth of leftover bits to good advantage.

Olive oil

2 cups of mixed and matched ingredients, approximately (see below)

8 or 9 eggs

1 tablespoon dry mustard

½ teaspoon cayenne pepper

1 or 2 dashes Worcestershire sauce

1 or 2 dashes Tabasco sauce

Salt

Freshly ground pepper

½ cup grated Parmesan cheese

Preheat the oven to 350°F.

In a 12-inch cast-iron skillet or some comparable stove- and oven-worthy pot or pan pour enough olive oil to cover the bottom generously; swirl the oil up the sides as well. Sauté in the oil approximately 2 cups' worth of any or all the following: finely chopped red or white onion, scallions, mushrooms, eggplant, zucchini, yellow squash, red, green, or yellow peppers, or potatoes. Along with (or instead of) the vegetables, you can also add cooked chopped sausage of any kind, or bits of ham, prosciutto, bacon, or chicken. You can also add, without cooking: canned corn or white or black beans (drained), minced black olives, leftover bean or other mixed vegetable salads, with as much vinaigrette drained out as possible. Chopped fresh basil, thyme, or parsley—2 tablespoons, or even a little more—are good herbs to use, and these needn't be sautéed either, just snipped in before adding the egg mixture.

Two rules only: (1) Definitely use one or another of the oniony ingredients, for flavor; and (2) don't use tomatoes—they're too watery, and the fritatta won't set as well.

Sauté whichever of the mixed ingredients you've chosen, then spread them evenly over the bottom of the skillet, sprinkling the fresh herbs on top. Set aside.

In a separate bowl, beat together the eggs, mustard, cayenne pepper, Worcestershire and Tabasco sauces. Use an egg beater, if you have one—they should be beaten together completely until just about frothy.

Pour the egg mixture over the mixed ingredients. Sprinkle with a little bit of salt (remember, the Parmesan is salty, too) and a lot of freshly ground pepper. Now sprinkle the Parmesan over the mixture, too.

Put the skillet in the preheated oven. Check after half an hour. It may take a few more minutes, but you should see the pie beginning to set. When the edges begin to brown and pull away from the sides of the pan, turn the heat up to broil. Broil until the Parmesan turns brown, too, and bubbly. When that happens, remove the fritatta from the oven and wait at least 10 minutes before serving, so that it sets completely.

Yellow Summer Squash Soup, Plus Other "Homemade" Soup Variations
To serve six

Some homemade soups take all day to make, some don't, and this one—which has any number of variations—doesn't. It's delicate, creamy (without adding too much cream, or even half-and-half), and both light and substantial at the same time. Incandescent yellow, it's also very pretty to look at. You can serve it hot or cold, and you can make extra to freeze.

The technique is one which lends itself very well to spin-offs: Basically you cook a big Spanish onion and the squash in a tiny bit of butter and (canned) chicken broth until they turn into a mush. Where al dente is the objective with most vegetables we serve these days, these vegetables get cooked to a mush, then pulverized smooth in a processor or blender. You don't boil away any vitamins or minerals, either, because the liquid gets pulverized, too. Then a little cream (or half-and-half) is added to sweeten it slightly and pull together the flavors; the cream also makes the color come to life. Salt, pepper, and that's it, unless you want to snip some fresh herbs on top.

For summer squash soup

Put the chopped onion, squash, and butter into a big pot, and pour in the chicken broth until it's about halfway to two thirds of the way up the vegetables, it doesn't really matter. It shouldn't cover them, though, because it *will* cover them once they cook and collapse into it. Bring to a boil and continue boiling gently until the vegetables are thoroughly mushy, about 20 minutes. When the mix is cool enough to handle, put it into a blender or food processor (it will take a couple of batches, so you'll need an extra bowl or something to keep the blended soup separate from the still-to-be-blended soup). When it's all blended, put it back into the pot, add salt and pepper to taste, then slowly stir in the heavy cream or half-and-half, 1/4 cup at a time, tasting each time; you want it to be pale yellow and taste good; 1/2 to 3/4 cup should do it, which isn't too bad divided among six people. Serve it with whatever you want.

1 big Spanish onion, coarsely chopped

2 pounds, or a little bit less, summer squash, stem end cut off and the rest of it coarsely chopped

2 tablespoons butter

One to two 10 1/2 -ounce cans chicken broth

Salt and freshly ground pepper

3/4 cup heavy cream or half-and-half, or a little of each, approximately

Herbs to snip on top of each bowl: dill, chives, chervil, parsley (optional)

Variations, all of which should be served hot

• *Curried corn chowder.* Gently boil a Spanish onion, coarsely chopped, in 2 tablespoons butter and one 10½-ounce can chicken broth until mushy. Drain 2 cans corn kernels, any size. Put corn and onion and broth into a blender or food processor, and blend until blended. Put it all back into the pot. Add more chicken broth if it's too thick to resemble soup, pour in a little heavy cream or half-and-half to pull it together, and season with salt, pepper, and curry powder to taste.

• *Broccoli soup.* Gently boil a Spanish onion, coarsely chopped, in 2 tablespoons butter and one 10½-ounce can chicken broth until mushy. In a separate pan, cook 4 or 5 big, coarsely chopped stalks and florets of broccoli until mushy or, better yet, use some leftover broccoli. (Don't cook broccoli with the onion, however, or it will impart a cabbagey taste to the stock.) Drain the broccoli, then put it into a food processor or blender with the onion, butter, and broth, and pulverize. Add more broth as needed to give it the texture of soup, then add a little cream or half-and-half to pull it together, and season with salt and pepper, and add, if desired, a little freshly grated nutmeg.

• *Cauliflower soup.* Same as broccoli soup, but with cauliflower. It may need a little extra broth, and cauliflower gets thicker when it's processed or blended. Skip the nutmeg, and snip in a little chives or parsley, which will make it look pretty.

• *Asparagus soup.* Same as broccoli soup, without the nutmeg.

• *Mushroom soup.* Slice a supermarket-size box of mushrooms coarsely, and boil gently with 2 tablespoons butter and one 10½-ounce can chicken broth until all is mushy. Puree mixture in a blender or food processor. Thin as needed with a second can of chicken broth, then smooth out and sweeten with heavy cream or half-and-half. Add salt and pepper to taste, and a jolt of sherry, if it's a very cold day and you want to be twice-warmed.

- *Pumpkin soup.* Gently boil a cut-up Spanish onion, 2 tablespoons butter, and 1 tablespoon fresh (or 1 teaspoon dried) leaves of thyme, and this time *two* 10½-ounce cans chicken broth until the onion is mushy. Blend the onion-stock mix in a blender or food processor, and return it to the pot. Start stirring in a 16-ounce can of pumpkin until the mixture thickens (you'll use most or all of it), then thin it out and sweeten it with heavy cream or half-and-half. Add salt and pepper to taste.

- *Earthy consommé.* Allow 1 cupful of really good chicken stock or broth per person, and 1 ounce of dried mushrooms, any kind, to serve six. Simmer the consommé with the dried mushrooms until the mushrooms have softened and their flavor has been imparted to the soup. (You can only tell by tasting.) Remove the mushrooms with a slotted spoon, unless you want to leave one or two in each cup, snip in some finely chopped curly parsley, grind in a little pepper, and serve in teacups with sandwiches, as a midafternoon snack (after a winter walk, say), or before supper on a cold night.

And so on, through spinach soup; leek and potato soup (clean the leeks well first, and cook them separately from the potato-onion-butter-broth mixture); sorrel soup; watercress soup; and any other soups you can think of.

Notes on Sources

*I*t's as much fun to read about food as it is to cook it, and reading is certainly less taxing. Great background reading includes: M. F. K. Fisher's *The Art of Eating* (New York: Vintage Books, 1976); *Much Depends on Dinner: The Extraordinary History and Mythology, Allure and Obsessions, Perils and Taboos of an Ordinary Meal*, by Margaret Visser (New York: Collier Books, 1986); *Kitchen Science: A Guide to Knowing the Hows and Whys for Fun and Success in the Kitchen*, by Howard Hillman (Boston: Houghton Mifflin Company, 1989); *James Beard's Theory & Practice of Good Cooking* (New York: Alfred A. Knopf, 1977): *The Artful Eater: A Gourmet Investigates the Ingredients of Great Food*, by Edward Behr (New York: Atlantic Monthly Press, 1992); *The Secret Life of Food: A Feast of Food and Drink History, Folklore and Fact*, by Martin Elkort (Los Angeles: Jeremy P. Tarcher, 1991); and *Elizabeth David Classics* (New York: Alfred A. Knopf, 1980). Two intriguing books that talk about the preventive and healing properties of food are Earl Mindell's *Food as Medicine* (New York: Simon & Schuster, Fireside, 1994) and Jean Carper's *Food—Your Miracle Medicine* (New York: HarperCollins, 1993).

As for cookbooks, everyone needs one that covers the how-to-boil-an-egg basics. I've turned to Irma S. Rombauer and Marion Rombauer Becker's *The Joy of Cooking* (Indianapolis: Bobbs-Merrill, 1973) more times than I care to think about. I can trace my attitude toward cooking directly to Peg Bracken's *The Compleat I Hate to Cook Book* (New York: Bantam Books, 1988). The two books cited in the text itself are *Darling, You Shouldn't Have Gone to So Much Trouble*, by Caroline Blackwood and Anna Haycraft (London: Jonathan Cape, 1981), and Barbara Kafka's *Microwave Gourmet* (New York: Avon Books 1991), the latter of which will be a great help to anyone confronted with a microwave for the first time.

Other than that, I've read and used and learned from dozens of cookbooks over the years. If I were stuck on a desert island, however, with only two cookbooks to keep me company, I'd take Alice Waters's *Chez Panisse Menu Cookbook* (New York: Random House, 1982) and *Wolfgang Puck Cook-*

book: Recipes from Spago, Chinois and Points East and West (New York: Random House, 1986). These books pique the imagination as much as they do the appetite, and they've helped set the high standard for the way we aspire to cook today, given the bounty that, thankfully, is available to so many of us.

A c k n o w l e d g m e n t s

$\mathcal{I}$’ve been lucky in the kitchen to find friends to cook *with* as well as friends to cook *for.* I’d especially like to thank Christopher Idone and Jason Epstein, cooking pals for years, both of whom have taught me a lot about food and creative ways to put it together and present it. It was over the course of several dinners with Carolyn and Stephen Reidy that the idea for this book came about, and my thanks to Carolyn, who found a truly welcoming home for it at Simon & Schuster. Working with Marilyn Abraham, my editor, has been immensely gratifying. Her knowledge, enthusiasm, and friendship touched the book on every page. (To say nothing of the fact that Marilyn’s husband, Sandy MacGregor, successfully tested the apple tart recipe and found that it works fine with frozen puff pastry.) I’m grateful, too, as always, to my friend and agent Binky Urban, whose encouragement over the years has been unfailing. Thanks are in order as well to Mary Flower, for her insightful copyediting, to Aviva Goode for her attentive help, and to Mark Gompertz, publishing friend from afar.

I’m grateful, too, to my husband, Michael Shnayerson, discerning taster (and critic!); to Susanna Porter, who can make a cook quake by forever claiming not to like garlic and then eating it anyway every time; to Gully Wells, who was especially enthusiastic about the project (and gave me my first food-writing assignment); to Melanie Fleishman, for reading the first draft. Thanks, too, to Suzanne Hamlin, Suzanne Jones, and Peter Trias, for their help with dessert. And to my mother, the first cook I ever met, whose forbearance throughout countless early and messy experiments involving chocolate chip cookie dough is still a source of wonder to me.

Index

Index